Poodles

Amy Fernandez

BARRON'S

Acknowledgments

This book could not have been written without the experts who generously shared their knowledge: Doris Cozart, Lucille Perzan, and Vicki Fierheller.

Thank you to my editor, Angela Tartaro.

About the Author

Amy Fernandez is a member of the World Dog Press, former president of the Dog Writers Association of America, a regular columnist for *Dogs in Review* and *Top Notch Toys*, and a regular feature writer for *Dog World* and the *AKC Gazette*. She is a founding member of the Xoloitzcuintli Club of America and has been editor of the *Xolo News* since 1986.

Amy has authored several books, including *Training Your Dachshund* (Barron's Educational Series, Inc., 2008), *The Chihuahua Bible* (Barron's Educational Series, Inc., 2009), *The Poodle* (TFH, 2008), and *Dog Breeding Is a Fine Art* (Ltd. Editions Media, 2002), for which she received the Maxwell Award for Best Reference Book of 2003 and the prestigious DWAA Presidential Award for Excellence. She is also a three-time winner of the Elsworth Howell Award, the 2006 winner of the Robert Cole Award, and the 2008 winner of the APDW Arthur Frederick Jones award for best long feature.

In addition to writing, Amy also has a passion for art. She is an award-winning artist and illustrator of dog-related books, articles, and breed standards. Samples of her work can be viewed online at *www.amyfernandez.net*.

All information and advice contained in this book has been reviewed by a veterinarian.

A Word About Pronouns

Many dog lovers feel that the pronoun "it" is not appropriate when referring to a pet that can be such a wonderful part of our lives. For this reason Poodles are referred to as "he" in this book unless the topic specifically relates to female dogs. This by no means implies any preference, nor should it be taken as an indication that either sex is particularly problematic.

Cover Credits

Shutterstock: front cover and back cover.

Photo Credits

Norvia Behling: pages 48, 73, 81, 162; Seth Casteel: 8, 16, 86, 146, 154, 166; Kent Dannen: page 37; Cheryl Ertlet: pages v, 5, 11, 12, 24, 28, 39, 47, 59, 105, 140, 145, 169; Jean Fogle: pages 20, 41, 61, 112; Sharon Eide Elizabeth Flynn: pages 7, 126, 142, 160; Paulette Johnson: pages iii, 45, 92, 109, 117, 118, 131, 152; Pets by Paulette: pages vi, 15, 135; Sherpa Pet Group, LLC: page 57; Shutterstock: pages i, 32, 52, 83, 97, 102, 111, 159, 170; Kira Stackhouse: pages 35, 70, 155; Connie Summers: pages 18, 27, 51, 54, 63, 64, 68, 75, 78, 88, 90, 98, 107, 120 (top, bottom), 121 (top, bottom), 122 (top, bottom), 123 (top, bottom), 124 (top, bottom), 125 (top, bottom), 129, 130, 132, 133 (left, right), 137, 149, 156.

All inquiries should be addressed to:
Barron's Educational Series, Inc.
250 Wireless Boulevard
Hauppauge, New York 11788
www.barronseduc.com

ISBN-10: 0-7641-6348-5 (Book)
ISBN-13: 978-0-7641-6348-7 (Book)
ISBN-10: 0-7641-8678-7 (DVD)
ISBN-13: 978-0-7641-8678-3 (DVD)
ISBN-10: 0-7641-9799-1 (Package)
ISBN-13: 978-0-7641-9799-4 (Package)

Library of Congress Catalog Card No: 2010003409

Library of Congress Cataloging-in-Publication Data
Fernandez, Amy.
    Poodles / Amy Fernandez.
        p. cm. — (Barron's dog bibles)
    Includes index.
    ISBN-13: 978-0-7641-6348-7
    ISBN-10: 0-7641-6348-5
    ISBN-13: 978-0-7641-8678-3
    ISBN-10: 0-7641-8678-7
    1. Poodles. I. Title.
    SF429.P85F473 2010
    636.72'8—dc22   2010003409

Printed in China

9 8 7 6 5 4 3 2 1

CONTENTS

CONTENTS

oodle images are imbedded in popular culture, typically used to symbolize fancy show dogs and pampered pets. But the multifaceted Poodle is far more versatile than this image suggests. When Poodles first achieved popularity, it was widely assumed that companion Poodles, truffle Poodles, performing Poodles, working Poodles, and the glamorous corded Poodles of the show ring were separate breeds. It was hard to believe that one breed was capable of succeeding in such an incredible range of endeavors.

Dog lovers eventually accepted the fact that Poodles deserved credit for all of these accomplishments, and the diversity of their admirers is no less amazing. Over the centuries, Poodles have attracted fans from every walk of life. If Marie Antoinette, Oliver Cromwell, Winston Churchill, and Gertrude Stein ever met, they would have no trouble striking up a conversation about their beloved Poodles. This is a dramatic testament to the Poodle's wide-ranging appeal.

Poodles were declared obsolete in the nineteenth century. In spite of that prediction, their popularity soared to new heights in the twentieth century. In Poodles, people saw the potential for a sled dog, a military dog, an obedience dog, and a therapy dog. There is no question that Poodles will keep pace with mankind and continue proving their mettle in sports and vocations we cannot yet imagine. At the same time, they have never wavered from their original purpose, earning a well-deserved place in our hearts as priceless companions. This book will give you a better understanding of the Poodle's fascinating heritage and varied talents. Most important, it will assist you in providing the best care for your best friend.

Chapter One

All About Poodles

Not long ago, Poodles were so rare, they bordered on extinction. The idea that they would one day become the most popular dog breed was unimaginable. The Poodle emerged in the Middle Ages, a time when hunting was elevated to an aristocratic pastime characterized by pageantry and fast hounds. Poodles, however, were developed for far less thrilling pursuits. The Poodle's job was to help lone hunters secure the family dinner. Hunting waterfowl not only lacked glamour and excitement, it was cold, wet, tedious, and extremely demanding. Before the invention of firearms, nets were the most common tool used to hunt birds. Subsistence hunters rarely had the resources to maintain multiple dogs, so water retrievers needed to be versatile. Along with retrieving game from freezing water, they were often called upon to track, flush, and drive prey into nets. These were valuable services, but dogs were not specifically bred for any of these tasks until the thirteenth century.

History and Development

By the Middle Ages, falconry or hawking was a popular form of sport hunting all over Europe. It required dogs that would look to the hunter for direction and willingly cooperate rather than act on instinct. Until then, hounds and mastiffs had been the primary hunting breeds, and their drive to hunt was triggered by the sight or scent of prey. Spaniels were developed to work with falconers by tracking game and helping birds bring down and hold prey. This required skill, timing, and, most of all, teamwork. In order to create specialized hawking dogs, breeders focused on traits that all dogs possess to some extent. Foremost among these was the ability to read human signals and the social drive to respond to them.

Ancestors of water retrievers became known as *oysel* (hawking) dogs and *dogs da rete* (netting dogs). Both were used to breed dogs specifically for hunting waterfowl. The earliest descriptions of *Canis aviarius aquaticus* (curly coated waterfowl retriever) come from twelfth-century Iberia. Water retrievers became the favorites of fishermen and sailors, and, thanks to them, these breeds spread from Iberia to Continental Europe by the sixteenth century. Their ubiquitous presence was documented in art and literature, and they became known by regional names such as *perro de agua* in Spain and *barbonne* in Italy. In Britain they were simply called rough water dogs. Eventually, distinct regional breeds of water retriever emerged, such as the Portuguese Water Dog, the Dutch Wetterhoun, the Irish Water Spaniel, the Tweed Water Spaniel, the Llanidloes Welsh Setter, the Curly Coated Retriever, the Russian Pod Laika, the Barbet and the Caniche in France, and the Wasserhund and the Pudel in Germany.

The Caniche takes its name from *cane*, a French word for duck. It descended from an older type of waterfowl retriever, the Barbet. During the 1700s the Barbet and the Caniche were gradually separated into two distinct breeds. Many waterfowl retrieving breeds are now extinct, and others are rare. Only the Poodle remains well known and highly popular.

A century later, British breeders made significant contributions to Poodle development, producing a uniform type from the plethora of regional varieties that existed at that time. They were also responsible for the dramatic improvements in coat and colors that were noted in the breed by the end of the nineteenth century.

When the working Poodle arrived in Britain in the 1700s, the breed was already acknowledged as Europe's premier water retriever. However, the habitat of Britain's waterfowl was fast disappearing as fens and marshes were drained, fenced, and paved in the name of progress. Within a few decades, waterfowl hunting was no longer a viable means of subsistence. Poodles were still used for this work in some parts of Europe, but from a British perspective, Poodles had lost their traditional function. "There are certainly less Poodles employed now for sporting purposes than there used to be and the difference between the number to be seen now and in the past arises simply from the fact that the majority of marshy lands are being reclaimed and cultivated and the Poodle's occupation will soon be gone entirely, as well as that of our own water spaniels" (*Dogs of the British Isles*).

Breed Truths

How Did the Poodle Get Its Name?

There is some debate regarding when the term *poodle* first came into use. It's generally agreed that the name was derived from the German word *pudel*. The Swiss naturalist Conrad Gesner used *pudel* to describe water dogs in 1555. In *The Miniature Poodle Handbook* (1960), Gerald Massey argues that *pudel* came into common usage through a series of inflammatory political pamphlets published in Britain in 1643. Historians will continue debating this point, but it's safe to say that Poodles began to emerge as a definite breed within this general time frame. References to Poodles in *Hunger's Prevention: or The Whole Arte of Fowling by Water and Land* by Gervase Markham leave no doubt that they were widely regarded as the premier water retriever by 1621, when the book was published.

FYI: What Is the French Poodle?

Today the Poodle is designated as the national dog of France. In fact, the breed was concurrently developed and refined in several parts of Europe, including Germany, Russia, and Britain. Although Poodle development was not confined to France, a definite type emerged there in the eighteenth century.

During this period, French breeders perfected multiple Poodle varieties. They were at the forefront of hunting dog development at this time and were the first to use Poodles as gundogs. The wealthy and powerful French court of Louis XIV (1638–1715) also set trends for the entire continent, including preferences in pets. As a result, elaborately coiffed pet Poodles were closely associated with the French court. Elaborate Poodle trims evolved in France because French craftsmen perfected the first precision grooming tools, which made it possible to sculpt and shave detailed patterns into coats. According to *Hutchinson's Dog Encyclopedia*, "The Curly, however, has always been more popular as a pet, and is what is known as the 'French' Poodle."

By the time dog shows and kennel clubs emerged in the 1870s, all water retrievers, including Poodles, were considered obsolete. This led to one of the first major quandaries for the newly established purebred classification systems. The Poodle was created as a hunting dog, but he was rarely used for this work. As a result, the Poodle became one of the first breeds to be designated variously as Luxury, Companion, or Non-Sporting. This designation implied that Poodles no longer performed any useful function, which was certainly not the case. Within one hundred years of the Poodle's creation, he had proven his worth in roles that early breeders could not have foreseen.

During the same era that Poodles were retrieving birds from Europe's lakes and rivers, they also enjoyed enormous popularity as performing dogs and pets. In 1867 the canine expert Stonehenge described "two grand classes of modern Poodles—one of which is still strictly sporting, and one which should include performing, companion, and toy Poodles—and each of these two classes comprises several different types...In fact, one may say, as a very general rule, that the Poodle in England is almost universally either a performing dog or a mere pet, or a lap or companion dog according to his size, but he is rarely employed as a sporting dog" (*Dogs of the British Isles*). Stonehenge may have termed them "mere pets," but Poodles had found a secure niche as adored companions of Europe's most powerful rulers.

Famous Performing Poodles

Amazing performing Poodles have delighted audiences since the seventeenth century. Troupes of trained dogs became extremely popular attractions in the nineteenth century, when changing social dynamics created a huge public demand for affordable, accessible forms of entertainment. Most of these acts consisted of acrobatic balancing and jumping routines and poodles excelled at this kind of trained dog show. With elaborate costumes and a variety of props, the best shows featured a repertoire of skits. Poodles dressed as firemen rescued Poodle victims in nightshirts from mock burning buildings. Poodles dressed as soldiers stormed a tiny fort defended by an opposing platoon of Poodle resistance fighters. One especially impressive show featured a formal banquet where well-dressed Poodle lords and ladies were seated at a table and served by Poodle maids and butlers.

These shows were enormously popular, but some of the most famous trained Poodles performed without the aid of props, costumes, or a supporting cast. One of the most celebrated was *Munito*, a Standard Poodle from Italy. In the 1890s, he was billed as *"The Learned Dog."* *Munito* proved his point by playing cards, dominoes, and chess. It was widely reported that he could read, write, and count. Undoubtedly, many spectators were thoroughly convinced of this after watching his remarkable show.

It required a substantial commitment of time and effort to train Poodles to this level, maintaining them in tip-top condition, and to create the elaborate stage sets and costumes. Trained Poodle acts were in high demand for centuries, and in some cases they became a viable family business.

The fascination with highly trained Poodles has continued into modern times. Poodles have appeared in countless films, in roles ranging from glamorous accessories to major characters. Thanks to their unmatched visual appeal and acting skills, Poodles will likely continue to fill this specialized niche.

Fun Facts

Aristocratic Poodle Owners

Marie Antoinette	Louis XIII
Kaiser Wilhelm	Louis XIV
II, Emperor of	Louis XV
Germany	Louis XVI
Henri II	Louis XVII
Henri III	Louis XVIII
Henri IV	Charles X

Poodle Coat

Ironically, the Poodle's most notable feature, his wash-and-wear coat, is now considered the ultimate symbol of canine decadence. The image of an elaborately coiffed Poodle is ubiquitous, but it creates a very misleading impression.

By the nineteenth century, nearly every region of Europe had cultivated some type of Poodle. Because the breed had been crossed with everything from Maltese to Sheepdog, Poodle coats ranged from wooly, to silky, to wiry. In spite of this diversity, a harsh, curly texture was acknowledged as the preferred Poodle coat. The recognition of this type as correct may have derived from the evolving understanding of functional coats. Harsh, textured coats not only dry quickly, they cord, which provides natural

FYI: The Truffle Dog

Poodles also developed a specialized niche as truffle finders. Dogs were first used for this work in Spain about three hundred years ago. The first truffle Poodles, bred for scenting ability, came from Germany. As the price for truffles soared to astronomical levels, truffle hunting became a major industry, and expert truffle finders were in high demand.

Truffle hunting required intelligence, patience, and a keen sense of smell to locate the fungus growing underground. Many dogs could be trained to sniff out truffles, but Poodles were regarded as the finest truffle hunters because they could be trusted to unearth the cache without damaging the pricey fungus. Lines of truffle-hunting Poodles were bred especially for this work. They were generally medium sized, with light-colored or parti-colored coats, as truffle hunting was highly secretive business done under cover of darkness.

protection against weather and underbrush. Softer woolly or silky coats will simply mat. Poodles from Russia and Eastern Germany were celebrated for their wonderful thick, harsh coats. "So decided is the tendency of the German Poodle's coat to cord, that even if you should comb it out (an almost impossible task), with a few hearty shakes it divides into separate locks, and in a few days is so felted as to almost defy the comb again" (*The American Book of the Dog*).

FYI: Poodle Trims

The AKC Poodle standard permits four trims:

- Poodles under a year old are shown in a puppy clip.
- Adults can be shown in the continental or English saddle clip.
- Poodles exhibited in non-regular classes can be shown in a sporting clip.

These are far from the only Poodle trims. A shorter version of the continental clip, similar to a traditional hunting trim, is known as the working continental clip. The most popular trims for pets are the retriever or kennel clip and the lamb clip.

Another popular style, the bikini clip, is also known as the ponjola, the summer clip, the Miami, or the clown clip. Also popular are the teddy bear, featuring more intricate hand scissoring, and the town and country and Dutch trim, which require a great deal of detailed clipping and scissoring.

These Eastern European dogs were genuine working Poodles. They were required to spend many hours outdoors in cold, damp weather, alternately plunging into freezing water, sitting quietly behind a blind or punt, or snaking through sharp underbrush to retrieve prey. A decorative coat would have been pointless in this environment. Their coats were supremely functional. They dried quickly to minimize loss of body heat, and they could be grown out for added protection in cold weather or trimmed short when extra protection was not needed.

The custom of clipping the face, legs, and hindquarters of water retrievers is centuries old, but it was subject to enormous variation. In his 1621 book, Gervase Markham explained that trimming Poodles was recommended for dogs that were used extensively in water or for hunting in hot weather. Removing part of the coat provided a compromise of protection, maximum mobility, and cleanliness. He advised against trimming dogs that were worked in the winter or used only for hunting on land.

Fun Facts

In the eighteenth century, Poodles were used to smuggle valuable handmade lace into Belgium in order to evade onerous customs fees. The lace was wound tightly around the dog's body, hidden by his dense, curly coat.

Fancy presentation evolved from this tradition, but it soon took on a life of its own. "During the reign of Louis XIV the Poodle became a fashionable pet in France and a lucrative trade was practiced along the banks of the Seine by Poodle barbers who ingeniously shaved various patterns on these long-suffering animals, including true lovers' knots and monograms" (*The Book of the Dog*). The basic lion clip eventually evolved into a standardized pattern known today as the continental clip.

The Evolution of Poodle Hairstyles

For many centuries, there were no conventional trimming patterns. Poodle grooming styles were influenced by fad, fashion, and utilitarian needs. Poodles were coiffed according to their owners' personal taste and grooming skills, as these historical descriptions attest:

> Poodles are denuded of coat in a variety of fantastic fashions: The muzzle is made bare, except near the nose, where what is called the "moustache" is left; from the middle of the back they are shaved, down the thighs, to the hock. In some cases a ruff round the hock is left, and the leg below that shaved—and the forelegs similarly treated; in other cases the long, corded curls are left from hock and knee downward; the docked tail is shaved halfway or more, and a huge, ugly tassel is left to dangle from the end of the stump. Some fanciers leave a tuft of hair growing in the middle of the thigh. (*British Dogs*).
>
> Before leaving [the subject of] coat, I may mention that fashion has ordained that the Poodle shall be shaven and shorn to pattern, this varying in detail in accordance with the particular taste of the owner, but in the main providing for a lion-like mane and body covering of hair, the loins, face, and legs being shaved, except for tufts of hair left here and there. These sometimes take the form of the owner's crest or coat of arms. . . . The standard states "if non corded . . . it is strongly recommended that the traditional lion clip should be adhered to." (*Show Dogs: Their Points and Characteristics*).

Fun Facts

In addition to elaborate trimming, topknots, and ribbons, nineteenth-century pet Poodles were commonly adorned with special Poodle bracelets, thick bands of silver worn around the pastern joint.

The need for officially sanctioned, standardized Poodle trims did not become a major issue until the popularity of corded Poodles began to wane after World War I. Trimmed and shaved Poodles had always been popular as pets, but they were rarely seen in the show ring.

When Poodles first became popular in Britain, coats were invariably corded. Most of these dogs were imported from Eastern Europe, especially Poland. The public was fascinated by their appearance, and an entry of corded Poodles virtually guaranteed spectator attendance at a dog show. In many cases, the length of the cords exceeded the height of the dog, and they had to be banded or tied to prevent them from dragging on the ground. Cording a coat and keeping it in top condition was incredibly challenging. Breeders lived in fear of dampness, mange, fleas, and hot spots. The cords had to be carefully protected, and a special hair dressing was applied regularly to prevent them from breaking. Although the Kennel

Club prohibited the use of artificial substances in coats, corded Poodles were exempted from this rule, presumably because this style of presentation had predated the rules.

By the turn of the century, fanciers began to realize that the demands of keeping a corded coat in good order were seriously interfering with Poodle popularity. They also began to question whether these complicated hairstyles really were in the breed's best interest. A few daring exhibitors began showing Poodles without cords, known as curly Poodles. Shows began offering divided Poodle classes for corded and curly dogs. Eventually, this grooming division was eliminated and size classifications became the status quo for Poodle exhibition.

The curly Poodle coat was, at first, championed as the natural, easy-care alternative to excessive grooming. Ironically, curly Poodle grooming evolved into an art in the nineteenth century, thanks to the introduction of sharp clippers and shears. For centuries, shaving with an open razor had been the only method of removing hair close to the skin. This remained a highly specialized skill until the 1870s, when the invention of the safety razor offered a safer and less expensive alternative. Still, Poodle grooming remained a painstaking job until the invention of manually operated clippers a few decades later. Until then, the perfect finish and fine detailing that now characterize Poodle grooming were almost impossible to achieve.

Breed Truths

Within a few years of the invention of manually operated clippers, shaving and trimming were a mandatory aspect of curly Poodle presentation. It became almost as technical and complex as the former demands of corded Poodle grooming. Nevertheless, by the 1930s, the corded Poodle had disappeared from the show ring, and all Poodles were shown in variations of the lion clip. Revisions in the breed standard in 1978 brought a few corded Poodles back into the show ring, but they have never regained their former popularity.

Today, all official Poodle trims include a topknot. The original purpose of tying a bright ribbon onto the Poodle's head coat and tail was utilitarian rather than decorative. The top knot ensured that the dog would have unobstructed vision when hunting. More important, this colorful decoration helped hunters to differentiate their dogs from the quarry. This was crucial when black was the predominant Poodle color.

Development of Toy, Miniature, and Standard Varieties

The Standard Poodle is the oldest of the three varieties, but both Miniature and Toy Poodles have been documented by artists, including Albrecht Dürer and Francisco Goya, since the sixteenth century.

Tiny Poodles, weighing as little as four pounds, were known as *Der kleine Pudel* in Germany and *Petit Barbet* in France. In most respects they resembled their larger counterparts, although some had a long, fine, silky coat. It is theorized that their tiny size was the result of crossbreeding between Poodles, Maltese, and Toy Spaniels. For this reason, diminutive Poodles were generally regarded as mixed rather than purebred. Despite this, their tremendous popularity encouraged breeders to establish them as distinct varieties. Both large and small Poodles were exhibited at early dog shows, which included classes for large working Poodles, little pet Poodles, and even performing Poodles.

A type of Toy Poodle, sometimes called the White Cuban, achieved great popularity in England in the eighteenth century. Some White Cubans were imported from Cuba, hence the name. However, it is unlikely that the breed originated there. Most experts believe that the White Cuban was bred from a combination of German or French white corded Poodles and Maltese brought to Cuba by European traders and settlers. It is probable that these dogs also played a role in the development of the Havanese.

England's Queen Anne became a devoted fancier of the White Cuban and owned a number of them. Her introduction to the breed came via a royal performance by a troupe of trained dogs of what was known as *The Ball of Little Dogs*. As Rawdon Lee noted in his 1897 book, *A History and Description of the Modern Dogs of Great Britain and Ireland*, "These dogs danced, two of them, with the grandiloquent titles of Marquis of Gaillerdain and Madame de Poncette, showing extraordinary training by the manner in which their movements kept time and cadence with the music which accompanied them." Despite their widespread popularity, there is no evidence that the modern-day Toy or Miniature Poodle traces back to the White Cuban or the aristocratic pets of the French court.

Breed Truths

In many countries, Poodles are divided into four sizes:

Standard	(45–60 cm)
Medium	(35–45 cm)
Miniature	(28–35 cm)
Toy	(24–28 cm)

The Miniature Poodle was created by selectively breeding smaller Standards, and the Toy was developed in the same manner from the Miniature. However, this was a lengthy process. Miniatures and Toys did not attain their present degree of uniformity until the twentieth century. At first, Miniatures were shown alongside Standards in the same classes. These two sizes were not officially divided into separate varieties until 1931. Until then, only one Poodle represented the breed in the Non-sporting Group, and the larger dogs generally did most of the winning.

The refinement of the Toy Poodle was also a complicated process. For many decades, the American Kennel Club (AKC) classified Toys as a separate breed rather than another Poodle variety. Because of this, interbreeding Miniature and Toy Poodles was technically crossbreeding, and therefore prohibited by AKC regulations. In 1943 the Toy Poodle was reclassified as a third variety of Poodle and Toy and Miniature Poodles could then be inter-

bred. This change was directly responsible for the improvements of balance and proportion in the Toy size.

The Poodle in America

The first Poodles arrived in America from England in the late 1800s. Most of these dogs were Standard size and black, white, or brown in color. They were among the first breeds recorded in the AKC studbook, which suggests that Poodles were considered a viable purebred at that time. The first Poodle recorded by the AKC was Czar, registered in 1887, and bred and owned by W. Lyman Biddle of Philadelphia, Pennsylvania.

The breed remained fairly obscure for a while; AKC records reveal that only one Poodle was registered in 1890. America's first Poodle club was formed in 1896 but disbanded three years later, leaving a legacy of the first official AKC standard for the breed. Poodles continued to grow in popularity, and a second club was founded in 1913. It was dissolved in 1927, at a time when many fanciers began losing interest in the breed.

Only 34 Poodles were registered in 1930. During these years, dedicated breeders such as Helene Whitehouse Walker came on the scene. Walker diligently promoted the breed, and imported high-quality dogs from England, including the famous Ch. Nymphaea Jason, who became the first Poodle to win the Non-sporting Group at Westminster.

The present-day incarnation of the club, the Poodle Club of America, was founded in 1931. The following year, 45 Poodles were AKC registered, and this number jumped to 105 in 1933. In large part, this resurgence of interest was due to the importation of beautiful Poodles from European kennels, such as the Labory Kennel in Switzerland. Foremost among these imports was Int. Ch. Nunsoe Duc De La Terrace. This dazzling white Standard was imported from Switzerland to America by Mrs. Sherman Hoyt, the breeder of Blakeen Poodles. His stellar show career included, in 1935, the first Westminster Best In Show for a Poodle. It was also the first time that a woman handler (his owner) had achieved this win.

These dogs not only refocused attention on the breed through their impressive show wins, their progeny raised the bar for Poodle quality in America. By 1950, the Poodle ranked 18th in AKC popularity, and by 1960 Poodles surpassed all other breeds in AKC registration statistics.

Poodle Popularity Over the Years

Poodles reigned as the most popular AKC breed from 1960 to 1982. No other breed comes close to this record of 23 years in the top spot. Since 1982, Poodles have consistently ranked in the top ten and are presently the ninth most popular of AKC's 173 breeds.

Writing in 1867, the noted canine authority Stonehenge feared that Poodles were soon headed for extinction: "Let poodles be rescued from the oblivion into which their breed seems to have fallen of late; it is a great mistake to allow such a valuable breed to become extinct—and extinct it certainly will soon be if no effort is made to rescue it from neglect and indifference" (*Dogs of the British Isles*). In part, the breed's low nineteenth-century approval rating was the result of their cleverness. Poodles were judged by the company they kept, and they had a longstanding reputation as the preferred companions of smugglers, poachers, and itinerant street performers. "A few years ago, if you told a 'doggy man,' either in this country or England, that he owned a Poodle he repudiated the charge immediately, and felt deeply insulted, as these dogs were deemed fit only for the circus or for mountebanks" (*The American Book of the Dog*). Poodles eventually overcame this unfair characterization, but they have retained their unshakable reputation as the premier performing dog.

Obedience trials have been instrumental in showcasing the Poodle's intelligence and trainability. These events have been a popular feature of dog shows for more than seventy years. They owe their

FYI: Poodles for Defense

America's first military canine training program, *Dogs for Defense*, was established on March 13, 1942, thanks to the determined efforts of Alene Erlanger, breeder of the famed Pillicoc Standard and Miniature Poodles. *Dogs for Defense* originally intended to obtain dogs, train them, and turn them over to the Armed Services. The group's ambitious plan was to supply 25,000 dogs to the U.S. Army, starting with Pillicoc Poodles and dogs recruited from Erlanger's fellow breeders. At first, any breed was accepted, but the list was soon narrowed to 32 breeds, Standard Poodles among them. Subsequently, the Army's Quartermaster Corps took over training and Dogs for Defense focused solely on procuring dogs for military service. In December of 1942, the group announced the need for 125,000 dogs for the Army, Navy, Marines, and Coast Guard.

A technical manual published in 1943 described the qualifications for each acceptable breed including those for the Standard Poodle.

"The Standard Poodle as a military dog presents a far different appearance from the traditionally landscaped Poodle seen at a dog show. He is clipped all over for Army work, and his coat is allowed to grow out to a length of 1 or 2 inches (2.5–5 cm), either all over, or with the face and feet clipped bare. Thus cut down, the Poodle looks like a medium-sized retriever. He stands from 20 to 25 inches (50–63 cm) high, weighing from 50 to 75 pounds (23–34 kg). His coat is tightly curled, very dense, of any solid color. He is a sturdy, squarely built dog, active and poised . . . Special traits [include an] unusual ability to learn rapidly, good retention, patience, agility, versatility, courage, keen nose and hearing." Poodles proved to be fearless, hardy war dogs, and grooming requirements were their only drawback.

In late 1943, the acceptable list was cut to 17 breeds, still including Standard Poodles. Although Poodles never saw active service overseas, they were used as sentries to guard U.S. defense plants, military installations, and coastal areas throughout World War II.

existence to the determined efforts of one Standard Poodle breeder, Helene Whitehouse Walker. Walker established her Carillon breeding program in the early 1930s. Through her contact with English breeders, she learned of formal obedience tests being held at British shows at that time. In October 1933, she designed America's first obedience test at an AKC show in Mount Kisco, New York. A second test was held in September of the following year, at the Somerset Hills Kennel Club in New Jersey. She continued organizing tests and demonstrations with her Poodles until finally, in 1936, the AKC approved the first formal obedience regulations based on her recommendations.

The first weekend that official AKC obedience competitions were offered, six dogs earned Companion Dog (CD) titles, including five Standard Poodles. In 1937, Ch. Carillon Epreuve became the first Poodle to earn all three obedience titles, CD, Companion Dog Excellent (CDX), and Utility Dog

(UD). Bred by Walker, she was trained and handled by Blanche Saunders, who later became a famed obedience trainer and author in her own right.

Poodles have proven to be equally adept at newer competitive sports and can earn AKC titles in agility, obedience, rally, hunting, canine good citizen, and tracking. Poodles can also earn Working Certificates (WC and WCX titles) through the Poodle Club of America.

Physical Characteristics

A Poodle can be described as a combination of a sturdy, athletic sporting dog and a regal aristocratic pet. There is no such thing as a perfect dog, but structural soundness and correct proportion are essential for any Poodle, whether he is a pet, a show dog, or a working retriever.

All three sizes should be squarely built, never appearing heavy and coarse or fragile and spindly. Even so, various combinations of long backs and short, stumpy legs are found in all three sizes. Ideally, a Poodle's height at the top of his shoulders should equal his body length.

A Poodle should have a long, well-proportioned neck. It should be graceful as well as strong enough for retrieving work. His back should be sturdy and level. Grooming can disguise faults such as dips and tilts, but they will nonetheless interfere with his ability to move efficiently. His tail should be carried high and straight. It is customarily docked, although no precise length is specified. It is never carried low or curled, or curved over the back. The Poodle's legs should be long and straight. He should have small, oval-shaped feet with well-arched toes, thick footpads, and short nails. Flat, splayed feet are a very serious fault because they compromise his ability to work. In the AKC standard, the Poodle's gait is described as "sound, effortless, light springy action." It also says that the Poodle is well proportioned with "revealing, proud carriage" and an "air of distinction and dignity." If all the pieces fall into place as they should, this is exactly what your Poodle will display on the move.

Toy Poodles measure 10 inches (25 cm) or less at the shoulder and weigh 4 to 6 pounds (2–3 kg). Miniature Poodles measure 10 to 15 inches (25–38 cm) at the shoulder and weigh 12 to 20 pounds (5–9 kg). Standard Poodles measure at least 15 inches (38 cm) at the shoulder. Typically, females are 22 to 25 inches tall (56–63 cm), weighing 40 to 50 pounds (18–23 kg), and males are 24 to 27 inches (61–67 cm) tall, weighing 60 to 70 pounds (27–32 kg).

Head and Expression

The Poodle's head is long, lean, and breathtakingly elegant. His moderately round skull is approximately the same length as his long, well-defined foreface. His muzzle tapers delicately and should never appear blocky or pointed. His eyes are dark, oval, and wide set to create an alert, intelligent expression. They should never be large, round, protruding, or squinty and should always be several shades darker than his coat color.

Nose, lips, eye rims, and nails should be black. The only exceptions are brown and café au lait-colored dogs, who should have liver-colored noses, eye rims, lips, and nails, and dark amber eyes. Apricot and red Poodles may have liver-colored noses, eye rims, and lips. Amber-colored eyes are permitted but not desirable.

His long ears are fan shaped and held close to the sides of his head. They should be long enough to reach the tip of his nose, although his coat often gives the impression that they are much longer. They are set onto his skull at eye level or lower.

The Poodle's teeth should be set in a scissors bite, meaning that the top incisors closely overlap the bottom incisors. If the bottom jaw protrudes beyond the upper, it is known as an undershot bite. If the upper jaw is notably longer than the lower jaw, it is termed an overshot bite. If either the upper or lower jaw is crooked or the teeth do not meet precisely, it is known as a wry bite. Dentition problems will affect a Poodle's expression and occasionally lead to dental-related health issues.

Although the Poodle's head features are clearly described in the standard, all sorts of variations exist in the breed. One of the most common incorrect variations is sometimes described as a "toy type" head. It is characterized by a very round skull, tiny ears, short muzzle, and large, prominent, round eyes. At the other extreme you will find dogs with long, flat, narrow greyhound heads. Another prevalent faulty head type is characterized by wide, bulgy cheeks and a heavy muzzle that is squared off rather than tapered at the tip.

Chapter Two

The Mind
of the Poodle

Poodle Personality and Temperament

Poodles are affectionate, fun loving, and willing to please. All of these traits stem from their instinctive sensitivity to human emotion. Their uncanny ability to empathize with us has made them beloved companions for centuries. However, this level of sensitivity is a double-edged sword.

Your Poodle is receptive and responsive. He will bond with you readily and demonstrate a strong desire for your approval. His need to please you will also cause him to react strongly to any indication of your disapproval. He may also become overly protective or clingy and demanding of your attention. These, and other, natural Poodle tendencies can pave the way to behavior problems such as separation anxiety, neurotic attention seeking, or inappropriate defensive aggression.

It's much easier to anticipate the realities of Poodle temperament if you understand how and why these personality traits evolved. Because Poodles quickly came to fill so many roles, their traditional purpose as a working breed is sometimes overlooked. As early as 1845, the canine historian William Youtt noted, "The Poodle was originally a water dog, but its qualities as a sporting dog are seldom recognized by its owner" (*The Dog*).

The Poodle's Heritage as a Water Retriever

When Poodles first emerged as a breed in the sixteenth century, water retrievers had already been used in Europe for three centuries. Several distinct breeds eventually developed, but they all shared certain crucial traits:

- Hardiness, stamina
- A harsh, densely curled waterproof coat
- Excellent swimming ability
- Keen intelligence and problem-solving skills
- A responsive, eager-to-please temperament

Along with certain physical abilities, water retrievers required specific mental traits. They had to be resourceful in order to resolve unanticipated complications that occurred during a hunt. Equally important was staunch determination. Many dogs lack the drive to continue working at a difficult problem under adverse conditions. A water retriever also had to be attentive. This was essential because, rather than working with a pack of like-minded, instinctively driven hounds, waterfowl hunting required teamwork with another species. Water retrievers also had to possess the somewhat contradictory traits of infinite patience and responsiveness. They were expected to remain alert without fidgeting, barking, or charging at the slightest movement. Supreme self-control had to be combined with lightning-fast reactions to retrieve prey with unfailing accuracy and no hesitation.

In short, his demanding work required excellent memory and learning ability, instinctive sensitivity to environmental cues, and a strong social drive. Over the centuries several breeds of water retrievers were used, but Poodles excelled in these qualities.

Poodle Intelligence and Trainability

Poodles are consistently rated among the most intelligent breeds. They boast an astounding track record of success in competitive sports such as obedience. They also consistently earn rave reviews from amateurs and professionals in activities ranging from therapy work to dogsledding.

The underlying reason for the Poodle's amazing versatility is his unrivaled ability to form learned associations. This is a great aid to training. You might need to go through a routine 20 times before many dogs learn to sit on

BE PREPARED! Common Training Misconceptions

Many books describe training as a clear-cut, predictable process. Unfortunately, Poodles generally do not read these books. As a result, owners may become frustrated and disappointed if their dog's behavior does not conform to conventional advice.

Maintain realistic expectations. Because Poodles are so intelligent, owners may underestimate the time needed for training. Keep your expectations reasonable, especially if you are training a puppy. Every dog is an individual and will require varying amounts of time and practice to learn new concepts. Factors such as maturity, previous training, and individual temperament will influence his learning rate. Make sure that your Poodle has mastered a skill or behavior before moving on to a new one, and don't expect too much too soon. For instance, it is tempting to give a puppy free run of the house after a few days of successful housetraining. This can be an invitation to disaster if the behavior has not been adequately reinforced.

Take responsibility for your training errors. Effective training also depends on your ability to get the point across. It takes practice to accurately evaluate your dog's body language and clearly communicate your wishes through properly timed commands and rewards. As a rule, Poodles are smart enough to figure things out despite inept training. However, skillful training certainly has a dramatic impact on a dog's learning curve.

Be imaginative. Poodles are fast learners, but every dog is a bit different. They do not respond equally well to the same techniques. If your Poodle seems baffled by your efforts, don't assume that he is being difficult. Try a different approach. Poodles are very good at learning complex tasks, but it's helpful to break them down into manageable steps when first presenting them. Don't be tempted to rush through training. Your Poodle will become stressed and confused, making you more impatient and frustrated.

Don't view training as a task to be finished and forgotten. Training is part of your ongoing relationship with your dog. His ability to constantly learn also means that he will reevaluate learned information and debate its continuing relevance. For instance, you may assume that your Poodle is perfectly well trained to come when called. However, if you forget to reward him when he does, he may think twice about whether it's still worth the effort. A less intelligent dog might simply respond as usual, without giving the matter much thought.

command. A Poodle may learn this after four or five repetitions. They also possess excellent problem-solving skills. Poodles quickly identify a challenge and actively seek a solution. They can easily adapt to changing factors in their environment. Just like their ancient canine ancestors, Poodles will find a niche and happily settle in.

On the surface, this sounds wonderful. A dog who learns quickly and effortlessly, and easily adapts to your routine, would seem to qualify as the ideal pet. But, like most things in life, there is more to this ideal than meets the eye. Living with a Poodle is an intense experience.

Because he is so good at noticing and remembering details, your Poodle will learn your daily routine in no time at all. Rather than simply observing, he will actively participate. As a result, you may begin to suspect that he can read your mind and foresee your every move. He will have no trouble anticipating when it is time for you to go to work, make dinner, or take him for his walk. He will also figure out when it is safe to sneak off and have some fun because you are distracted with a phone call or your computer.

Most dogs have a limited ability to generalize. Once they learn a specific concept, they rarely expand the parameters. This is not the case for Poodles. They are programmed to look for new information and use it. Therefore, you must be aware of the messages you communicate via training. For example, if you reward him for jumping onto his grooming table, do not be surprised if he tries jumping on the kitchen table. If he gets lucky, and lands next to a ten-pound roast, don't be surprised if he develops amazing powers to levitate onto every surface above eye level.

Like all water retrievers, Poodles readily form mental maps of their environment. This is useful when it comes to locating a duck in a marsh, and it is equally handy for picturing the location of his favorite items in your home. You may forget where you left your keys, but your Poodle will never forget where you left his treats. He may also figure out how to open the tricky latch on the cupboard door.

Poodles possess an active curiosity about their environment. Many dogs outgrow this inclination as they mature, but Poodles remain ready and willing to experiment and devise new strategies throughout their lives. This explains their amazing capacity to master complex training, as well as their ability to recall and repeat successful behaviors learned via trial and error. Do not assume that this is something you can control. Many dogs ignore the household buzz happening around them, but not Poodles. Everything he is exposed to in his daily environment provides a constant stream of information to sharpen his problem-solving skills. Unfortunately, you and your Poodle may not always agree on the problems that require a solution. Opening the latch on the kitchen cupboard will solve his perceived problem of a daily snack shortage. Prying the screen out of the window and going for a stroll will solve his problem of being bored.

Highly intelligent breeds like the Poodle are also far less resistant to boredom. If you don't provide mental challenges for your Poodle, he may develop bad habits like barking, chewing, or raiding the trash for entertainment. This is just the beginning. Don't underestimate the things that a bored Poodle might try. If you notice that your Poodle is developing an annoying habit, your first course of action should be to reevaluate his daily routine.

At this point, you may be thinking that Poodles are far more complicated than you imagined, and no one in their right mind would take on such a challenge. Take heart. A few simple, commonsense steps will prevent most Poodle misbehavior, and ensure a good relationship between you and your dog.

Breed Truths

Sports and activities are a great way to keep both you and your Poodle entertained. However, many trainers advise concentrating on one activity at a time. They caution that dogs may become confused by conflicting training cues, and for many dogs this is true. They fixate on one response to a particular cue and cannot generalize this behavior to encompass multiple situations. This is not the case for Poodles. You can train your Poodle to track on a 20-foot lead and harness, heel for obedience off lead, and gait on a show lead in the conformation ring. He can differentiate between the equipment and environment for these activities.

Tips for Building a Solid Relationship and Preventing Behavior Problems

Provide regular training. The breed's reputation for intelligence and trainability encourages the belief that Poodles are preprogrammed for good behavior. In reality, highly intelligent breeds require more training because they are naturally inquisitive. Many dogs have a fairly limited time span for learning new skills. Once they have outgrown their learning phase as puppies, they do not easily assimilate or utilize new information. This is not the case for Poodles. From puppies to seniors, Poodles can and will constantly seek new information and put it to use. If you do not keep your Poodle's mental resources channeled in the right direction, he may use them in ways you didn't anticipate.

Helpful Hints

The Pack Leader

More than anything else, your Poodle needs an attentive, benevolent pack leader. It's true that dogs are instinctively attuned to the dynamics of pack behavior, but this concept can be misinterpreted. Your role as pack leader does not require dominating your pet through bullying, punishment, or forceful training. Spontaneous behaviors like jumping up to greet you, dashing through doorways, or sleeping on furniture may indicate misbehavior. However, they are not signs of dominance or your Poodle's desire to usurp the role of pack leader.

This concept becomes easier to understand if it is examined from an evolutionary perspective. Dogs and humans formed a bond thousands of years ago because of the striking similarities in our social behavior systems. Both species are hardwired to respond to social cues because group living greatly enhanced our odds of survival. Successfully defending territory, raising pups, and procuring food required the cooperation of the pack. Even though dogs no longer need a pack to survive, they remain highly attuned to social cues and instinctively seek the acceptance of a pack.

From a practical standpoint, this means that your dog will look to you for leadership. He wants to remain part of your family pack, and he wants his pack to remain harmonious. To achieve this he will happily follow your rules. It's your job to communicate this information clearly, consistently, and kindly.

Whether you are working with a Toy or a Standard, introduce your Poodle to basic commands at a young age. Puppies are capable of learning at seven weeks. Consistent training not only satisfies his natural desire to work, it provides essential guideposts to help him understand your expectations.

Avoid regimented training. Training is important, but don't overtrain your Poodle. Because they absorb information quickly, they easily become bored with repetitive drilling. If that happens, he will devote his mental energy to finding an escape route from the tedium. No amount of coercive training will revive his interest in this endeavor. You will be faced with the job of starting from square one with an entirely different approach.

Spice up his training with variety. Regularly introduce new challenges to exercise his natural versatility. For instance, if you sense that your Poodle is getting a bit bored with traditional obedience work, a class in agility or tracking could be a welcome change of pace. Rather than repetitiously practicing familiar commands, build on his learned skills. For example, when he has mastered *sit*, use this as the first step to teach a trick like *shake hands* or *sit up*.

Provide regular breaks from routine training as well as

regular exposure to other forms of mental stimulation. Long hikes to explore a new area will satisfy his natural curiosity as well as his canine instincts. Accompanying you on daily errands or visiting friends will satisfy his need for social interaction.

Setting Boundaries

It's essential to be patient and positive, but this doesn't mean that you should never say no to your Poodle. He will never understand basic manners or boundaries of acceptable behavior unless you set and enforce limits. Without these skills, his life will be filled with needless complications and stressful encounters. Your role as his pack leader is to impart these essential concepts through thoughtful guidance. Consistent rules should be incorporated into his daily routine.

Providing mixed messages or failing to reinforce household rules is a sure recipe for misbehavior and anxiety disorders. Regardless of intelligence, no dog can adapt to constantly shifting expectations. This is a major reason why dogs develop neurotic coping strategies. For instance, if you do not want your Poodle jumping on you for attention, you must respond the same way every time he does this. You may find this exuberant greeting delightful when you come home from a hard day at work. On the other hand, this may not seem quite as wonderful at 6 A.M. when you are tackled by a frenzied furball on your way to the shower. You cannot expect your dog to understand that different rules are in effect at 6 A.M. and 6 P.M.

Consistent household rules will also prevent much of the bad behavior that Poodles can pick up through accidental learning. Accept the fact that your Poodle is going to know when you are thinking of going out for the day or getting ready to prepare his dinner. Unless you teach him behavior guidelines, you may end up with a dog who drives you crazy every time he suspects that a walk, snack, or car ride is imminent.

Control Resources

Indulge your Poodle to your heart's content as long as you keep one rule in mind. Whether it is a cookie, a walk, or a belly rub, make him work for his rewards rather than simply giving in to his demands.

In other words, your Poodle should receive his food, treats, toys, and playtime when *you* decide. He should be fed at a scheduled daily time, not because he is barking and demanding to be fed immediately. Your response should make him understand that his behavior plays a role in the process. Reinforce the idea that he is expected to politely wait while you prepare his food. If he is permitted to bark and jump, grab food from your hand, or growl at you while he eats, you're pretty much telling him that he is in charge of this process.

This approach also applies to walks and playtime. Your reactions can teach him that it is perfectly acceptable to run wildly through the house

barking, or impart the message that he must wait calmly while you get your keys, coat, and attach his leash. If you alternately reward and ignore the same behavior, you can expect equally random responses from him. Consistently insist on appropriate behavior and never fail to reward it. When he does slip up, you won't need to resort to punishment. Simply withhold his expected resources as well as your attention.

Poodles are too smart to constantly repeat a behavior that does not work. If sitting politely earns a pat on the head and a bowl of food, he will quickly ditch the bark-and-lunge strategy. Calmness, firmness, and consistency are far more effective than attempting to assert control through forceful measures.

Pay Attention

It's important to remain attentive to your Poodle's behavior and reactions. Thanks to their intuitive awareness of human emotions, Poodles are extremely responsive to your moods, both good and bad. For instance, a loud argument between human family members may cause a Poodle to do something completely out of character because he has interpreted this as a threat.

Since your Poodle takes his cues from you, you must be aware of the behaviors you encourage through praise and attention. Simply remembering to reward his good behavior is often enough to keep him on the right track. Whether or not you are actively attempting to train him, your Poodle constantly observes you and learns from your behavior. He works to please you, and he is sensitive to your impatience or anger.

PERSONALITY POINTERS
Attention Seekers

It's important to discourage attention-seeking behavior. Poodles are particularly sensitive to rewards that involve human attention. Less motivated dogs might make a few attempts to get attention. If these strategies fail, they give up and go back to their chew toys or naps. Poodles are not only highly motivated they quickly form cause-and-effect associations. It is therefore quite easy to unintentionally encourage annoying behaviors like whining, pawing, or nibbling your hand, as these actions reliably get your attention.

A great deal of canine behavior is subtle and easily overlooked. Because they are retrievers, many Poodles have a natural tendency to mouth your hand or the cuff of your pants. If your Poodle persistently does this, be aware of your response when it happens. You may routinely respond by petting him, without even realizing that you are encouraging something that has the potential to become an ingrained bad habit.

During training, it is crucial to be aware of the signals you send through your vocal tones, gestures, and facial expression. There is no inherent satisfaction for him in retrieving a dumbbell or showing off clever tricks. These behaviors are motivated by his desire to please you. He may not get it right every time, but he is trying.

Factors outside of your control can also alter the rules governing his behavior. For instance, varying aspects of his environment can have a major impact on his perceptions and habits. Thanks to his natural energy and curiosity, it's not unusual for a Poodle to venture into situations that ultimately leave him frightened or confused. Even though he needs opportunities to investigate, allowing him to explore without supervision can have negative consequences. It is your responsibility to ensure that these experiences are safe, positive, and beneficial. As hunting dogs, Poodles are highly sensitive to their environment and may react suspiciously to anything surprising or unusual. In a situation like this, he will instinctively look to you, his pack leader, for reassurance and direction.

If you are not paying attention, you may not even notice that his attitude has changed from curious to fearful. Unless you intervene by calming him, distracting him, or removing him from the situation, his self-protective instinct will kick in. If this happens frequently, his response will become habitual. You may find yourself with a snappy, sharp Poodle and only yourself to blame.

Don't leave him on the defensive, but don't make the mistake of going to the other extreme either. Poodles can become very dependent and clingy if they are over-protected. Because they are so responsive, it is very easy to begin treating your Poodle like a child rather than a dog. Smothering him with attention can discourage his natural desires to be a dog. Poodles are naturally resourceful and famed for their ability to keep themselves entertained. However, a well-behaved Poodle is a combination of genetics *and* training. Don't take it for granted.

Positive Reinforcement Training

All canine species, including domestic dogs, tailor their behavior in response to social signals. Dogs are adept at interpreting social cues from other species and at evaluating social interactions based on potential risk and reward.

This is why so many aspects of dog training seem effortless. If your Poodle is rewarded for doing something, it's very likely that he will do it again. This applies equally to intentional and unintentional training. Jumping on the kitchen table may entail some courage, but if it results in a tasty treat, he will quickly categorize it as a manageable risk. Once he makes this learned association, he will retain the idea despite variable success. Most launches onto the kitchen table may earn him a few overripe bananas from the fruit bowl, but to him, this still qualifies as a successful survival strategy.

If you walk into the kitchen and discover him devouring the dessert course you planned to serve to your dinner guests, your wrath will probably cause him to think twice before trying this again. He will certainly be more careful about getting caught, but don't assume that he has abandoned the idea. Remember, learning implanted via positive reinforcement is far more durable than information learned via negative reinforcement. On the surface, these seem to be equally power-

CAUTION

Separation Anxiety

Separation anxiety is a common behavior problem in Poodles. They easily form strong attachments to their owners, and it's only natural for owners to reciprocate. At the same time, your Poodle should have regular opportunities to spend some time alone. Without these experiences he will not be comfortable with the idea of being separated from you. This sense of dependence can evolve into separation anxiety. It's characterized by unreasonable levels of generalized fearfulness whenever the dog is left alone, or when he is separated from a particular individual. Without behavior modification, he will progressively become more clingy, demanding of attention, and resistant to spending time alone.

Correcting separation anxiety involves a complicated behavior modification process, sometimes in combination with drug therapy. Needless to say, prevention is far easier than a cure. Your Poodle's routine should accustom him to spending some time alone and learning necessary coping skills.

ful motivating factors. However, information assimilated through positive reinforcement more easily becomes a stable memory, which is an essential aspect of learning.

Until recently, the most common dog training method consisted of repetitious drills reinforced by verbal and physical corrections. It is not surprising that many dogs complied simply to avoid corrections. Some Poodles were trained successfully with this approach; others were so stressed that they simply shut down and refused to cooperate. Many more became bored or resentful, and as a result, training acquired in this way remained fairly unstable. Poodles have no trouble forgetting information learned through coercive training, because from a canine viewpoint, it has no long-term relevance. Drill training also had limited usefulness when teaching complex behaviors that require putting several ideas together, solving a problem, or dealing with varying factors. These situations require a strong motivation to work, rather than simple willingness to obey rote commands. For Poodles especially, forceful methods are counterproductive because they do not foster an incentive to work cooperatively, which is precisely what Poodles were bred to do.

Both humans and dogs respond to intimidation, as social signals are closely tied to our survival instinct. You can probably sense when someone is displeased with your behavior long before they decide to whack you in the head. When a situation escalates to this frightening conclusion, it rarely results in a useful takeaway message. Both dogs and humans are naturally programmed to avoid overt confrontation.

When you are displeased with your Poodle's behavior, a stern *no* followed up by withholding your attention is usually sufficient to get the message across. Problems arise when we are preoccupied with countless human issues and fail to notice the dog's social cues. At these times, it becomes very easy to unconsciously reinforce the wrong message.

When Dog-Owner Communication Fails

Communication is especially prone to fail when you are multitasking, and interaction with your Poodle becomes a secondary consideration. For instance, perhaps you arrive home from work and your Poodle is ecstatic. You can hear him barking when you pull into the driveway. As soon as you get in the door he rushes to greet you, jumping, barking, and racing around the house in delirious joy. If this over-the-top greeting is not the behavior you want from him, you should not respond in a positive manner. It's easy to momentarily forget this rule if you are looking through the mail and checking your phone messages rather than giving him your full attention. Instead, you may pat him on the head and let him out so he can share his joy with the neighbors.

Eventually, your preoccupation with dinner and phone calls is interrupted by a sound like a cannonball being thrown against your backdoor. At the same time, you vaguely hear your neighbor yelling about the barking dog in your yard. Suddenly, you realize that your Poodle is annoying the neighbors, destroying your screen door, and shredding the unread newspaper he discovered on the porch. You immediately bring him in and read him his rights.

His joy is instantly replaced by dread. He runs upstairs to hide. Satisfied that you have gotten your point across, you have dinner, watch a little TV, and stroll up to bed, where you immediately step in a pile of Poodle poo in the hallway. The dog is nowhere in sight. You eventually find him hiding under the bed in the guest room, which is normally off-limits for him. Now you are furious. He not only created havoc with the neighbors, he has sought revenge by having an accident in the hallway and venturing into forbidden territory.

Let's look at the evening's events from his point of view. He has been waiting for hours to see you, and when you arrive you reciprocate with attention, praise, and a run in the yard—even though you have previously decided that boisterous behavior earns none of these privileges. At this point, he is confused but happy, willing to take what life offers. After a few minutes of running wildly around, he wants to come back in the house for more quality time with you. You again change the rules, unintentionally ignoring him as you order dinner and check the TiVo. His frustration level mounts. He begins to bark, finds the newspaper, and tears it to shreds. When that does not work, he mounts an all-out assault on the door. So far, he has given no thought to his need to relieve himself and you have paid no attention to his activities in the backyard.

When you finally remember that you left him outside, you also assume that he did his business, since he was certainly out there long enough. In fact, he barely got started on that mission because he was preoccupied by this sudden revision of daily rules. It is too late now. Not only is he ordered into the house, the festive greeting he expected is replaced with the Spanish Inquisition. Negative reinforcement gains you some short-term success. Your Poodle quiets down and disappears for the moment. Once he takes care of the call of nature, he finds a remote hiding place.

At this stage of the game, your Poodle is thoroughly baffled by your behavior and simply worrying about his future status

Helpful Hints

Body Language Chart

Poodles are not only excellent at reading social signals, they communicate very well. Simply paying attention to your Poodle's body language and facial expressions will provide a great deal of information about his moods and intentions. The key to interpreting canine gestures is to examine the overall picture. Just like a remark taken out of context, a canine gesture can be misinterpreted. When making a determination about your Poodle's state of mind, observe the whole dog as well as any preceding actions.

PERSONALITY POINTERS
Poodle Body Language

Mood	Friendly	Curious or Excited	Playful
Head Carriage	Normal posture or tilted slightly upward	Erect or slightly tilted	Moving side to side or lowered and tilted upward
Eyes	Alert and attentive, soft direct eye contact	Wide open	Open wide, making direct eye contact
Ears	Alert, forward, relaxed	Alert, raised, or slightly angled to listen attentively	Alert, raised
Mouth	Closed, lips relaxed	Relaxed or slightly but open, teeth are covered by the lips	Relaxed or slightly open, but teeth are not visible
Body	Relaxed posture, weight evenly distributed on all four legs	Legs braced, neck arched, stretched posture, weight shifted to forequarters, standing tall	Relaxed in play postures, nudging with hips or paws, pawing at playmate, jumping up to spar or play bow
Tail	Wagging gently, held high	Carried high, wagging fast	Carried high, relaxed wag

in your pack. You are probably thinking that he is a thoroughly spiteful, ungrateful dog. This encounter is not likely to end well; more important, it can set the stage for a downhill slide in your relationship. From his point of view, his former friend can no longer be trusted. He will maintain his guard and think twice before initiating any interactions with you in the future.

A Better Approach
It is no secret that anyone—dog, human, or lab rat—will work much harder when motivated by a reward than by a punishment. This predictable response has been used in dog training and human interactions since prehistory. However, not until the twentieth century did researchers confirm that the expectation of a reward produces a powerful motivation to repeat

Apprehensive or Anxious	Fearful	Subordinate
Slightly lowered, neck turned	Lowered, turned away, rigid neck muscles	Low and turned to side, or persistently nuzzling dominant individual
Blinking or averted to avoid eye contact	Wide open, fixed stare, whites of eyes may show, pupils dilated	Averted, refusing to make eye contact
Pulled back, drooping	Pulled back against skull	Pulled back against skull
Nose licking, yawning, chattering teeth (all signs of displacement activity), drooling	Slightly open, tense jaw muscles, lips lifted and pulled back to bare front teeth	Lips pulled back in submissive expression resembling a wide, tense grin; obsessive lip licking or tongue flicking
Sitting or restless pacing, leaning on person for support, obsessively licking, self-grooming, or pawing the ground	Tense, trembling back arched in cowering position, or legs braced with weight shifted to rear to spring and run	Persistently nudging or pawing at dominant individual or rolling on back to show submission
Carried level with back or slightly lower	Tightly tucked	Tightly tucked

a specific behavior. Positive reinforcement studies conducted by researchers such as Konrad Lorenz and B. F. Skinner were first put into practice in the 1960s by dolphin trainers. Since the 1970s dog training methodology has also shifted to reward-based techniques, and the results have been phenomenal.

These methods work so well because the dog's behavior is motivated by positive expectation rather than fear of negative consequences. Positive reinforcement training also has the potential to modify instinctual behaviors that are normally resistant to conventional coercive methods. For Poodles, the primary advantage of this approach is obvious. Poodles were bred to respond to human interaction. Negative interaction, even if it is meant as a training tool, will undermine this instinctive bond. Training that strengthens this bond provides the foundation for a lifetime of learning and teamwork.

Chapter Three

How to Choose a Poodle

O nce you've decided that the Poodle is the perfect breed for you, how do you go about choosing your new pet? Your quest to find the right Poodle for you will raise a multitude of questions. Although they are charming, intelligent, and versatile, this doesn't guarantee that every Poodle will fit perfectly into your lifestyle.

What to Consider

When you start searching for the Poodle of your dreams, important considerations are sometimes overshadowed by other issues, like deciding on the color or sex of your new pet. Be sure to consider the following issues carefully.

Your Personality

Poodles have a well-deserved reputation as affectionate, joyful companions. Every dog possesses a unique blend of temperament traits, however, and it's important to find one that will complement your personality. Puppy buyers are usually advised to look for the boldest, liveliest puppy in a litter. This may not be the best idea if you are unprepared for a strong-willed, high-energy dog. A placid puppy may not have as much dramatic impact, but he is more likely to grow into a calm, temperamentally balanced adult. If possible, evaluate the overall temperament of the puppy's close relatives. Poodles bred from a line of obedience or conformation champions should display fairly consistent and predictable personalities. If a puppy's parents, cousins, aunts, and uncles are boisterous and energetic, this tells you what to expect from the puppy.

Your Experience as a Dog Owner

Poodles are often touted as the ideal breed for novice dog owners. They are portrayed as invariably playful, friendly toward other pets, and highly trainable. Depending on size and age, they can also be quite active and inquisitive. It's more accurate to say that a Poodle can be the ideal choice for

COMPATIBILITY Is the Poodle the Best Breed for You?

	Rating
ENERGY LEVEL	
Toy	● ●
Miniature	● ●
Standard	● ● ●
EXERCISE REQUIREMENTS	
Toy	● ●
Miniature	● ●
Standard	● ● ●
PLAYFULNESS	● ● ● ●
AFFECTION LEVEL	● ● ● ●
FRIENDLINESS TOWARD OTHER PETS	● ● ● ●
FRIENDLINESS TOWARD STRANGERS	● ● ●
FRIENDLINESS TOWARD CHILDREN	● ● ●
EASE OF TRAINING	● ● ● ●
GROOMING REQUIREMENTS	● ● ● ●
SHEDDING	●
SPACE REQUIREMENTS	
Toy	●
Miniature	● ●
Standard	● ● ●
OK FOR BEGINNERS	● ● ● ●

4 dots = highest rating

a novice if that particular dog has a companionable temperament. Levels of trainability and sociability vary within the breed. A puppy's personality is a combination of nature *and* nurture, and it is possible to damage the temperament of a well-bred, stable Poodle through neglect or improper training. If you are not confident about your puppy-raising skills, an adult might be a better choice. This minimizes training demands as well as speculation about the dog's personality.

Available Time for Dog Care

Poodles are consistently rated as one of the most intelligent breeds. Don't make the mistake of thinking this will be a time-saving factor. Poodles learn quickly, but this is not limited to formal lessons. Intelligent dogs constantly investigate their environment and seek challenges. In short order, a bored

or neglected Poodle will discover a multitude of ways to entertain himself, which may include unwanted behavior.

Your Expectations as a Poodle Owner

Most Poodles live their lives as devoted pets, but this can take many forms. As a rule, Poodles are happy to find their niche and contentedly adapt to any lifestyle. If your Poodle is intended as a companion, balanced temperament and good health should be your primary concerns. You should also be realistic about a dog's mental and physical potential. A Toy may not be the best choice for young children, and a boisterous Standard puppy may not be the ideal companion for your 90-year-old grandmother. If you are hoping to try your Poodle in dog sports or conformation, it's important to choose a dog bred with this purpose in mind. You should acquire your Poodle from a breeder who actively competes in your sport of interest. Not only are you more likely to get a Poodle with the mental and physical potential for this activity, you will have the benefit of a mentor.

BE PREPARED! Poodle Expenses

Adequately training and supervising your Poodle will also help you to avoid major expenses like carpet cleaning, floor refinishing, furniture repairs, and landscaping.

One-time costs
AKC registration: $20
Microchip: $35–$75
ID tag: $5
Crate: $30–$85
Collar or harness and leash:
   $20–$30
Food and water dishes: $20–$30
Dog bed: $30–$75
Basic grooming supplies
   (brush, comb, nail trimmer):
   $100–$150
Portable exercise pen: $45–$150
Baby gate: $50

Yearly expenses
Veterinary care (check up, heartworm
   testing, vaccinations, dental cleaning if needed): $350
Food: $250–$600

Grooming supplies (shampoo,
   conditioner, ear cleaner,
   toothpaste): $50–$75
Treats, toys, dog coats: $25–$200
Dog license (if required): $35

Optional expenses
Professional grooming: $45–$120
   per visit (every four to eight weeks
   depending on the dog's trim, coat
   quality, and lifestyle)
Equipment for DIY grooming (clipper,
   grooming table, hair dryer,
   scissors): $500
Doggy daycare: $15–$25 per day
Dog walker: $7–$15 per day
Training classes (eight-week session):
   $150–$175
Pet health insurance: $100–$200 per
   year

The Costs of Raising a Poodle

Many of the expenses associated with raising a Poodle are difficult to esti-
mate. Average costs for grooming and veterinary care vary depending on
where you live and the size of your Poodle.

In some ways, a Toy Poodle is more economical. He consumes less food,
and requires smaller, less expensive equipment; plus, grooming and boarding costs are usually lower. However, many costs—such as vaccinations,
microchips, and registration fees—are fairly consistent regardless of the size
of your Poodle. Most of these expenses are unavoidable, so you should be
prepared for them before acquiring a dog. During these economically challenging times, it's even more important to understand the financial responsibilities of pet ownership. On the other hand, sensible planning can help you
keep expenses to a minimum.

Most important of all, do enough research to ensure that you acquire a
healthy pet. Keeping your dog in good health entails regular checkups,
but this should be the limit of veterinary expenses for a well-bred Poodle.
Unfortunately, a poorly bred Poodle suffering from one or more chronic

health disorders can run up astronomical veterinary bills. Many pet health insurance plans do not cover corrective surgery or long-term medication in situations like this.

The Realities of Poodle Ownership

Poodles were originally bred as working partners for hunters. This genetic heritage dictates their need for attention, mental challenges, and physical activity. It's easy to underestimate these requirements. Don't forget that all three sizes were developed from the same gene pool and, therefore, possess the same general characteristics. Miniatures and Toys don't require as much exercise as Standards, but they are dogs in every sense of the word. They will resort to the same strategies as the Standard to cope with boredom and frustration.

Grooming

Unfortunately, some owners are attracted to this breed because they are seeking a maintenance-free pet. Drooling, shedding, and doggy odor are non-issues, but there is no avoiding the Poodle's need for frequent grooming. Whether you prefer a manicured or a natural tousled look, your Poodle requires regular clipping and scissoring. This can be done professionally

FYI: Hypoallergenic Breed Myths and Facts

Poodles are often recommended as a good choice for people suffering from allergies or asthma. Many breeds are touted as hypoallergenic, meaning that they are guaranteed not to trigger allergic reactions in sensitive individuals. In reality, no dog can live up to such a claim. Dead hair and dander are regarded as the major allergy triggers, and *every* dog, including Poodles, produces them to some degree. Proteins in canine saliva and urine also have the potential to trigger an allergic response in a susceptible individual.

Curly-coated breeds like Poodles are less likely to cause an allergic reaction for a couple of reasons. As a rule, they shed very little, and dead hair remains trapped in the coat until it is removed by brushing or bathing. They also have thinner, dryer skin, which produces less coat dander. Larger dogs inevitably produce proportionally larger quantities of dander, which makes a small Poodle a better choice for an allergy sufferer.

Keep in mind that even minute amounts of dander may cause an allergic reaction in a highly sensitive individual. Also, Poodle coat quality can vary significantly. Some Poodles shed more and produce higher levels of dander. This is more likely to be a problem in designer hybrid Poodles produced by mixing Poodles with breeds noted for extensive shedding.

every four to eight weeks. Or you can invest in a set of grooming tools and learn how to do it yourself.

Even though many owners opt to have their Poodles professionally groomed, this must be supplemented with coat care and maintenance in between visits. Certain trims will minimize grooming demands, but you should be prepared to handle basic chores like brushing, bathing, dental care, and nail trimming.

Ideally, Poodles should be brushed every other day and bathed at least twice a month. Unfortunately, every Poodle is not blessed with the ideal harsh coat texture. Soft, cottony coats require more attention because they pick up more dirt and are more prone to matting. Ears should be examined, and cleaned if necessary, each week. Depending on your Poodle's activity level, his nails will need trimming every week or two. Some Poodles are prone to eye stains and must have their faces wiped and dried daily to keep this under control. Your Poodle's teeth should be brushed several times a week.

Allergies

If you suffer from allergies and you are considering a Poodle, the first step is to consult an allergist. He or she can evaluate the severity of your allergies and advise you regarding the possibility of successfully living with a dog. If the doctor gives the go-ahead, the next step is to confirm that you can tolerate long-term close contact with a Poodle. You may feel confident about your ability to tolerate a Poodle, but this feeling is often influenced by

the desire to have a pet. If you purchase a Poodle and bring him home, you (and your family) will fall in love with him. Everyone will be heartbroken if you discover that you must return him a few days later because of an allergic reaction. Although you may feel fine after visiting a friend's Poodle in the local park, this is no guarantee. Arrange your own Poodle allergy test.

Ideally, you should arrange to spend time with a Poodle in your home for several hours. Make sure that the visit involves plenty of close interaction. Pet the dog, brush him, and have him sit on your lap. Since the dog will be the only new element in your environment, you should be able to quickly determine whether he is the source of an allergic reaction. If that isn't possible, visiting a Poodle owner may also provide a good test, but there is a greater possibility that you will be exposed to additional allergens.

HOME BASICS
Steps to Minimize Allergic Reactions

Brush and bathe your Poodle frequently with a mild shampoo to remove allergens from his coat. Vacuum rugs and furniture often, especially areas where your dog spends a lot of time. Better yet, choose rugs and furnishings made of non-porous materials such as vinyl, plastic, or leather. These are easier to clean and attract less hair and dander. Always wash your hands after handling your dog.

Choosing the Right Poodle

Toy, Miniature, or Standard?

Toy, Miniature, and Standard Poodles share many traits. Each variety also has some unique advantages as well as drawbacks.

The Toy Poodle is officially classified as a Toy breed, in contrast to Miniature and Standard Poodles which are members of the Non-sporting Group. An abundant coat can give a misleading impression of a Toy Poodle's actual size. Toys should not exceed 10 inches (25 cm) in height at the shoulder, but some are as small as 6 or 7 inches (15 or 16 cm). They normally weigh 4 to 8 pounds (2–4 kg) at maturity, making them easily portable and an excellent choice for small homes and apartments. Their moderate exercise needs can be satisfied with a couple of ten-to fifteen-minute daily walks. This is an indoor breed, but you should be prepared for an active companion. Unlike some Toy breeds, Toy Poodles are playful and athletic. This creates some dog-proofing challenges. As with any small dog, owners must be prepared to protect them from a multitude of potential hazards, both mental and physical. For instance, Toy Poodles have a reputation for being noisy. However, this behavior is often a response to justified anxiety. In many situations, a dog of this size is going to feel vulnerable and defensive.

Breed Truths

Beware of anyone who uses unusual size as a marketing ploy to sell Poodles. There are only three recognized sizes within the breed. Aside from the obvious, there are essentially no differences between the three varieties. Terms like *teacup*, *micro miniature*, or *royal standard* are meaningless designations used solely to inflate the value of oversized or undersized Poodles. Dogs that are dramatically smaller or larger than average may not be purebred.

The Miniature Poodle is an excellent choice for owners seeking a compromise between small, compact size and sturdiness. This variety measures between 10 and 15 inches (25–38 cm) at the shoulder, and weight can range from 12 to 20 pounds (5–9 kg). Miniature Poodles are small enough to adapt to an urban lifestyle as long as they have two or three fifteen-minute walks each day. They are fairly athletic and appreciate longer outings. They are great jogging and hiking companions, and a good choice for children. However, this is still a fairly small dog, and you must be prepared to use caution in places such as dog parks and busy streets.

Technically, any Poodle over 15 inches (38 cm) at the shoulder qualifies as a Standard, and the AKC standard contains no maximum size restriction. Most Standards are substantially larger than the Miniature variety, ranging from 21 to 27 inches (53–67 cm) in height. Females are typically smaller, weighing about 40 to 50 pounds (18–23 kg). Males are generally 60 to

70 pounds (27–32 kg), but large specimens can weigh 80 pounds (36 kg) or more. Standards don't require as much exercise as many comparably sized dogs, but they should have 45 minutes of brisk exercise daily. Despite their size, Standard Poodles are popular city pets, and a combination of long walks and free running exercise at dog parks can satisfy their needs. They are a great choice for active owners who enjoy rural pastimes and dog sports.

Don't expect your Standard to be an ornament. They are intense dogs, and they need strong leaders willing to provide emotional support, challenges, and plenty of personal interaction.

It's important to realistically appraise factors such as space limitations when selecting a Poodle. However, a large house or a fenced yard is far from the only important consideration. Regardless of his size, your Poodle needs daily attention. Some Poodles, however, require far more than others.

Poodle Colors

Black and white are the most popular Poodle colors, but they can also be found in shades of blue, gray, silver, brown, red, café au lait, apricot, and cream. Some colors normally change as a puppy matures. At birth, the coats of browns, reds, and apricots may range from almost black to deep chocolate. Silvers are usually black at birth. They begin to lighten at 8 to 12 weeks old, but may take up to a year to achieve their true adult color. Poodles should be a solid color, although shading is allowed.

The idea that certain Poodle colors are linked to temperament was widely accepted at one time. For example, black Poodles were believed to be more robust and intelligent. White Poodles were considered more frail and sensitive. Brown Poodles were labeled as nervous and erratic. Despite the longstanding prevalence of these myths, there is no evidence to prove a genetic link between coat color and personality.

Many breeders specialize in one or two particular Poodle colors; a more casual approach vastly multiplies the complications associated with producing correct color and pigment. Recessive colors like chocolates and silvers present the greatest challenges, but incorrect pigment, and eye colors and mismarked coats can crop up in any Poodle breeding program.

For all colors, an even tone throughout the coat to the skin is desirable. However, a slight variation, such as darker shading on the ears, sometimes occurs, and the AKC standard allows this for lighter colors such as cream and apricot. No Poodle color descriptions allow multicolored coats, which are regarded as a disqualifying fault. Parti-colored coats of two or more colors occur most frequently, but the disqualification also applies to variations such as tan markings on solid-colored coats. Although these dogs are disqualified from AKC conformation events, they may participate in AKC companion events and compete for United Kennel Club (UKC) conformation titles.

Breed Truths

Parti Poodles

Mismarked Poodles encompass a wide range of patterns and color variations. Most often, a small amount of color, usually white, appears on the chest of a solid-colored dog with no variation in skin color. Unusual color patterns typically crop up by accident in Poodle litters; serious breeders do not intentionally perpetuate them.

The UKC recently recognized Parti-Colored and Phantom Poodles, and they are now eligible to compete for UKC conformation championships.

According to the UKC, Phantom poodles are bicolored and must include typical markings on the muzzle, throat, forechest, legs, feet, and face.

Parti-Colored Poodles must exhibit a coat pattern of 60 percent white and 40 percent black, brown, or tan.

Male or Female?

Despite a prevailing belief that female Poodles are more affectionate and easier to train, there are no temperamental differences between the sexes. Male and female Poodles are equally intelligent and friendly. They are also equally likely to develop behavior problems if socialization and training are neglected.

FYI: The Best Age to Get a Puppy

Many training guides recommend acquiring a new puppy at seven or eight weeks of age. This advice is based on the belief that very young puppies most readily bond to a new owner and adjust to a new home. However, most Poodle breeders prefer waiting until their puppies are 9 to 16 weeks old before sending them to new homes. Puppies usually receive their first vaccination at eight weeks, but vaccine-induced immunity does not always develop immediately. Keeping the puppy for a few extra weeks ensures that he is larger, stronger, and better protected against common diseases. Interaction with his dam and littermates during these early weeks also improves his social skills to make a successful transition to a new pack. As long as the puppy has received regular social contact, he will be mentally equipped to adjust to a new home at any age.

Through no fault of their own, male Toy Poodles have an undeserved reputation for being especially difficult to housetrain. Toy dog owners are sometimes rather lax about housetraining their pets. This may result in territorial marking as an untrained male pup enters adolescence. Female Toy Poodles can also develop these unfortunate habits, which are easily prevented through supervision and training.

Likewise, problem behaviors like mounting and chronic barking can and do occur in both sexes. Bored or lonely Poodles often use these habits to offset anxiety or solicit attention. Because Poodles crave social interaction, even the negative attention of a scolding can be interpreted as a positive response.

Most behavior problems occur equally in both sexes in response to boredom, frustration, and lack of training or exercise. Rather than focusing on the dog's sex, look for a balanced temperament when choosing a Poodle to complement your personality.

Puppy or Adult?

It's easy to fall in love with the idea of raising a puppy, but you should also be prepared for the time and effort this entails. Socializing a puppy to strangers, housetraining him, and introducing him to grooming, car trips, and leash training, are long-term commitments. Puppies start out cute and charming, but they don't stay that way unless you invest time in training and socialization.

Housetraining may take six weeks to six months. Basic house manners must be consistently reinforced for three to six months. Socialization must be continued until adulthood. A puppy also requires consistent supervision to prevent him from getting into trouble or developing bad habits until he is reliably trained. If this sounds like fun, you are ready for the challenges of owning a puppy.

FYI: The National Parent Club

The Poodle Club of America website (*www.poodleclubofamerica.org*) features comprehensive educational resources for prospective buyers and new puppy owners. But providing breeder referrals and puppy care information is just one of the club's activities. The primary role of a national parent club is to safeguard the breed's welfare. The Poodle Club of America is responsible for writing and revising the breed's official standard, representing the breed's interests regarding AKC policies, funding genetic research, conducting health surveys, and promoting genetic testing to screen out health problems. The club also devotes resources to educating novice owners, breeders, and judges and rescuing Poodles in need of new homes.

Thanks to the breed's enduring popularity, there is never a shortage of Poodle puppies for sale. They can be found in the classified sections of newspapers, countless websites, and many pet shops. It is possible to find a great Poodle from any of these sources. However, your chances of success are greater if you have access to information about a puppy's ancestry and background.

For example, breeders routinely screen their dogs for genetic disorders. Some of these tests are done only once, and others must be updated annually. Recommended tests for Toy Poodles include OptiGen testing for progressive retinal atrophy, certification of hips and patellae by the Orthopedic Foundation for Animals (OFA), and annual CERF testing for eye disorders. Recommended tests for Miniature Poodles include OptiGen testing for progressive retinal atrophy, OFA certification of hips, and annual CERF testing for eye disorders. Recommended tests for Standard Poodles include OFA certification of hips, skin punch testing for sebaceous adenitis, thyroid testing, and annual CERF testing for eye disorders.

Dogs must be at least one year old before they can receive OFA patella certification and two years of age before OFA certification for hips. Results are graded as excellent (E), good (G), or fair (F). CERF eye exams must be updated every 12 months. Health test information for many AKC-registered Poodles can be accessed via the Canine Health Information Center (CHIC), a centralized canine health database maintained by the AKC and the Canine Health Foundation.

Finding a Poodle Breeder

Technically, anyone can call himself or herself a dog breeder. Breeders range from entrepreneurs who produce countless puppies solely for profit, to novices who breed their pets without knowing quite what they are doing. On

the other hand, serious breeders are motivated by the desire to improve the breed and produce puppies that conform to the standard. This is more difficult than it sounds. Consistently producing healthy puppies with proper temperament, athletic structure, and important Poodle characteristics requires incredible time, effort, and attention to detail. These are the breeders that you want to work with.

For serious breeders, this is a labor of love. They do everything possible to give their puppies the best start in life. Although every litter is intended to produce show-quality puppies, some will not make the grade. Details like coat quality, tail carriage, ear length, or eye shape will tip the balance. These puppies still possess the hallmarks of good breeding and devoted care. They receive the best food and veterinary care. They are raised in an enriching environment to foster their mental development and social skills. Purchasing your puppy from a serious breeder has another advantage. You will have a reliable source of information on training, grooming, and health care. If your breeder is unable to answer a question, he or she has access to a network of experts for advice.

The AKC is a good place to start searching for breeders in your area. You can contact the AKC by phone at (919) 233-9767 or by e-mailing info@akc.org. The AKC website (*www.akc.org*) contains a wealth of information for potential puppy buyers and new owners, in addition to breeder referral contact information (*www.akc.org/breederinfo/breeder_search.cfm*). Newly registered litters can be searched through AKC's online breeder classified listings (*www.akc.org/classified/search/index.cfm*)

The AKC can also help you locate Poodle specialty clubs in your area. All-breed dog clubs and training groups may be able to provide informa-

BE PREPARED! Long-Distance Purchases

Thanks to the advent of Internet research, the click of a mouse can put you in touch with Poodle breeders all over the world. Although it has become common-place, purchasing a puppy or adopting a rescue dog long distance is more compli-cated than doing so in person. A few precautions are recommended.

In addition to a contract, request references from verifiable sources such as vet-erinarians, certified trainers, or local or national dog clubs. Do not rely solely on information from a website. Speak to the breeder or rescue coordinator by phone at least once. Ask plenty of questions and think twice if the answers are not satis-factory.

Ask for pictures and detailed information, such as the puppy's pedigree and health records, pictures of the parents, recent photos, or (for a rescue dog) health and temperament evaluations.

Also use precautions when shipping your Poodle by air. If possible, arrange to have someone accompany the dog on the flight rather than shipping him as cargo. If cargo shipping is your only option, wait until the puppy is at least 12 weeks old. Book a direct flight even if it means driving to an airport farther from home. Avoid shipping on weekends, holidays, or during weather extremes, even if the airline will accept dogs for shipment.

tion on local breeders as well. The AKC website includes links to the Poodle Club of America, where you can find listings of breeders throughout the country.

Referral services will provide you with a list of names, but it is up to you to contact individual breeders for specific information on their dogs, prices, and business practices. Breeders come from widely varying backgrounds, but they should have one thing in common: an impressive depth of Poodle knowledge.

Don't hesitate to ask questions. Dedicated breeders will happily and skill-fully answer general questions, as well as specific questions about their background and technical questions about the breed. As a rule, breeders don't need much prompting to launch into a detailed discussion of Poodle type, structure, temperament, and function. Beware of breeders who evade complicated questions and focus on a litany of personal preferences.

As long as you make arrangements in advance, you should be able to visit breeders and see their dogs. Most likely, a reputable breeder will insist on meeting you before agreeing to place a puppy in your home. Be prepared to answer questions about your daily routine, family, and living situation. Some of these questions may seem intrusive, but it's the only way to con-firm that you are prepared to raise a puppy. You should similarly prepare your own list of questions. Breeders should willingly provide information on their health testing routine and husbandry practices. Inquire about their

puppy placement policies, and ask to see a copy of their sales contract. In addition to a contract, the breeder should provide the following information at the time of sale:

- Records of vaccination and deworming treatments the puppy has received and dates when additional treatments are due
- Food recommendations and a feeding schedule
- A list of recommended puppy supplies
- Basic advice on care, training, and grooming
- A registration certificate or application, or a written statement that registration will not be forthcoming. Pet puppies are usually sold with a spay/neuter agreement and an AKC limited registration, which renders any offspring of the dog ineligible for AKC registration. If registration papers are being withheld until the puppy is neutered, you should be informed of this prior to the sale.

Sales Contracts

A written sales contract is the best way to prevent misunderstandings that may arise from a puppy sale. This does not need to be six pages of legal stipulations and fine print. A straightforward document recording the details of the sale and mutually agreed terms protects the breeder, the buyer, and, most important, the puppy. Read the contract before you sign it. If you don't fully understand it, request an explanation. If you want additional written clarification on a particular point, ask the breeder to insert this into the contract. Along with a frank discussion prior to sale, a contract ensures that everyone is on the same page.

The contract should include the date of sale, a description of the puppy, and the agreed-upon price. It should also specify each party's obligations. This normally includes the seller's obligation to provide a healthy, purebred Poodle and the buyer's obligation to maintain the dog as a house pet and provide all necessary care to ensure his well-being.

Don't assume that these requirements are not legally binding. For instance, most contracts state that the puppy must be returned to the breeder if the buyer is unable to keep him for any reason. In other words, if you are going off to college next year and intend to place your Poodle with your parents, you should disclose this information prior to the sale. Don't be surprised if the breeder asks to meet your parents before agreeing to this arrangement. This may be inconvenient, but it is preferable to discovering that you have been sued for breach of contract because you transferred the dog to another party without the breeder's consent.

Every clause in the agreement should include the penalty for failing to honor that point. For example, the buyer may be obligated to return the puppy, without any refund forthcoming, if he is found to be living in sub-standard conditions. The breeder may be required to replace the puppy or refund the purchase price within 60 days of the sale if the puppy is found to be unhealthy. Most contracts stipulate that the buyer must have the puppy checked shortly after purchase to confirm good health at the time of sale. It should also fully explain the breeder's health guarantee. The guarantee may be limited to health problems arising within the first week or month, and it may or may not contain a provision for refund or replacement if the puppy develops a late-onset health problem.

Some contracts provide a grace period, ranging from three days to two weeks, during which the puppy can be returned for a full refund for any reason. Do not assume this to be the case unless it is specifically stated in the contract. If the puppy develops a health or behavior problem, the contract should specify a time period for the buyer to document the condition and for the breeder to provide a refund or replacement. In some states puppy lemon laws require sellers to compensate buyers for veterinary expenses if the puppy develops a major health problem. However, such laws vary from state to state. They may not provide any protection for out-of-state purchasers. Securing repayment for veterinary bills may entail filing a lawsuit in that state's small claims court. If the amount exceeds that limit, a civil lawsuit becomes your only option. You can file a civil action in your state, but don't be surprised if the defendant petitions for a change of venue requiring you to travel to that state to have your day in court.

FYI: Designer "Doodles"

In the past decade a wide range of cross-bred Poodles, known as Doodles, have become popular as pets. The concept of the crossbred designer dog originated with the Labradoodle, a cross between a Labrador Retriever and a Poodle that was invented in Australia in the 1980s. This breeding program was sponsored by the Royal Guide Dog Association in order to create a guide dog for allergy sufferers who could not tolerate breeds normally trained for Seeing Eye work.

Since then, distorted advertising has led to many misleading notions about cross-bred Poodles. The most prevalent belief—that they are consistently free of health and temperament problems—is based on erroneous assumptions about genetics. Stable, healthy parents produce stable, healthy puppies. This holds true whether the parents are of the same breed or differ-ent breeds. Good-quality Labradoodles are not unusual, but these dogs are the prod-uct of quality bloodlines and well-managed breeding programs.

However, the vast majority of designer dog breeders rarely have access to high-quality purebred Poodles. Serious Poodle breeders do not dabble in experimental breeding. This makes it less likely that stable, healthy dogs will be used to pro-duce designer Doodles. Crossbred dogs can suffer from any health or temperament dis-order that either parent may carry or pos-sess. If the sire or dam carries a detrimental gene, it can be passed on to their progeny. Again, this holds true whether the parents are purebred, mixed breed, or designer cre-ations. Designer dogs also tend to be quite unpredictable in regard to size, tempera-ment, energy level, and coat quality.

Most important, the contract should provide recourse to solutions other than a civil court action if either party is dissatisfied. Emotions can easily override common sense in these situations and a lawsuit rarely justifies the mental and financial toll—even if you come out on the winning side. Needless to say, it's far preferable to avoid this unpleasant possibility. If you do face the prospect of going to court to settle the matter, written proof of your agreement becomes your best defense.

Acquiring an Adult Poodle

If you are not prepared for the challenges of raising a puppy, an adult Poodle may be a better choice. Potential owners sometimes fear that an adult dog may not live long or bond to a new family. Poodles not only have a long life span, they are famed for their adaptability. With some breeds, old dogs really do have problems learning new tricks, but this is not the case for Poodles.

Breeders are often delighted to find caring homes for retired champions or show prospects that didn't quite make the mark. These dogs are trained, socialized, and acclimated to a household routine and usually adjust smoothly to a transition. An adult Poodle will need some remedial training in order to learn your routine, but this rarely equals the demands of training a puppy.

Rescue Poodles

Poodle rescue groups are a good source of adult dogs. Through a network of local rescue organizations, the Poodle Club of America (PCA) rescues and places unwanted Poodles. A listing of these groups can be found through the AKC and PCA websites.

Prior to placement, rescued Poodles are examined by a veterinarian and treated for any outstanding health problems. They are also vaccinated, neutered, and microchipped if needed. They are then placed in temporary foster homes with rescue volunteers. This home setting provides an opportunity to evaluate each dog's temperament, and institute remedial training if necessary, while he awaits permanent adoption.

Rescue Poodles generally adjust readily to new homes, and careful screening ensures a good match between dog and owner. Along with detailed questions, the rescue group may request a home check and meeting with family members and other pets. After placement, rescue volunteers also maintain regular contact to monitor the dog's progress and offer advice in case problems arise.

Rescue groups generally charge a fee of approximately $250. This helps to defray the costs of running a volunteer program and discourages people who are simply looking for a free purebred.

Shelter Dogs

Despite the best efforts of breeders and rescue groups, Poodles do turn up in animal shelters. These dogs can be challenging to accurately evaluate for

ACTIVITIES PAL/ILP Program

Don't assume that only registered Poodles can participate in fun sports such as rally or tracking. In many cases, you can obtain AKC registration for Poodles from an undocumented background, such as rescues and shelter dogs. The AKC enrolls approximately 3,000 dogs per year in its Purebred Alternative Listing/ Indefinite Listing Privilege (PAL/ILP) registration program. A PAL/ILP number can be used in lieu of an AKC registration number on entry forms for a variety of AKC events, including agility trials, junior showmanship, obedience, rally, tracking, and hunt tests (for Standard Poodles). Registration requires a non-refundable $35 fee, a veterinarian's certification that the dog is neutered, and two recent color photographs clearly showing the dog's head, facial characteristics, and profile.

Visit the AKC website for more information on the PAL/ILP program at *www.akc.org.*.

several reasons. It's often difficult to determine whether they are mixed-breed Poodles, poor-quality purebreds, or simply in unrecognizable condition because of neglect. It can also be difficult to accurately assess a dog's temperament. Shelter workers usually try to provide some information on a dog's personality based on short-term observation and some temperament testing. They do their best to offer advice and guidance to prospective adopters. However, this can be challenging if they have little or no background information on the dogs in their care. In a shelter environment, some dogs become hyperactive or defensive. Others become withdrawn in response to the stress and confinement. Some develop anxiety disorders. The dog's genuine personality may not emerge until he is moved to a less stressful environment.

Adopting a dog from a shelter often means saving a life. This is truly a good deed. You should also be prepared for a lifetime commitment. This may include retraining or lengthy behavior modification. Many dogs end up in shelters because of behavior problems that have gotten completely out of hand. Your adopted Poodle may need complete housetraining, a step-by-step introduction to household rules, or a challenging program of remedial socialization. Owners of shelter dogs commonly assume that the dog was previously mistreated and readily attribute any and all behavior problems to a past history of abuse. In reality, poor socialization is the primary culprit. Rather than coddling and overprotecting the dog, remedial socialization is often the best remedy. Separation anxiety is another common behavior problem of rescued dogs. They have trouble transitioning from a situation where they had no attention to suddenly becoming the center of attention.

If you encounter training or behavior problems with your rescued Poodle, don't hesitate to seek expert advice. Most problems can be resolved with the right approach.

Chapter Four

Caring for a Poodle Puppy

Your puppy probably arrived from his breeder with reams of instructions. Many facets of his care are straightforward. Feed him a recommended food at scheduled times. Choose a good veterinarian and don't miss his appointments for health checks and vaccinations. Provide daily grooming and exercise.

The most critical part of his upbringing, however, is less tangible. The decisions you make about your daily interaction will lay the foundation for his success or failure as man's best friend. Unless the crucial elements of mutual trust and understanding are firmly in place, your relationship will never be truly rewarding.

Reading and comprehending your Poodle's body language for effective communication is the first step in forming a successful bond. You must be able to recognize when he is feeling receptive, curious, fearful, or confused. This is especially important during his socialization period (up to 16 weeks), when new experiences have a tremendous impact on his developing personality.

Puppy Proofing

Before your puppy arrives, part of your home should be modified to remove obvious dangers and valuables from his reach. It will be impossible to keep him safe and out of trouble if he has access to the entire house.

He should be restricted from areas that are not puppy proofed, but it is equally important to include him in your daily routine. He should spend most of his time in a part of the home where he is exposed to plenty of household activity. Almost any room can be made puppy safe, but those with easily cleaned non-porous surfaces offer an obvious advantage. Certain features—like antiquarian books, potted palms, and drapery pull cords—are simply accidents waiting to happen. A puppy can become entangled in a looped window cord and strangle within minutes. Cords on drapes or blinds can be replaced with safety tassels or attachments to prevent loops from forming between the slats.

Valuables can be moved out of reach, and child safety products, such as toilet locks and baby gates, can resolve other potential hazards. However, safety gadgets can create a false sense of security about possible risks, many of which are not obvious to the untrained eye. Envisioning the room from your puppy's vantage point makes it easier to identify dangers and temptations in his path. Puppies are unpredictable, and the best safety measure is ongoing supervision. Remember your puppy's abilities and interests will change as he matures. The gate you installed to prevent him from falling down the stairs may become his favorite chew toy or climbing challenge a few months later.

Helpful Hints

Even the most attentive owner cannot watch over a puppy 24/7. You should prepare an area where he can be left safely when unsupervised. This might be a puppy pen or a partitioned area of your laundry room or kitchen. He should have access to a bed or crate, some safe chew toys, and water, so that he can be comfortably left there for a few hours. However, this area is not a jail cell meant for long-term confinement.

Your Puppy's New Home

Your puppy is not a blank slate. He already has a repertoire of social skills the day he arrives at your home. Puppies begin to initiate social interactions when they are three or four weeks old. By seven weeks, their ability to understand canine social gestures is well developed. They are also primed to absorb information from their environment. Your puppy's genetic heritage and survival instinct prompt him to investigate his environment and form social bonds. He has a natural desire to explore and learn during these weeks when his curiosity and learning potential are at their highest. This window doesn't remain open forever, so make the most of it. Puppies are bold and curious because, for their ancestors, survival hinged on developing the skills necessary to fit into the pack. In contrast, caution is the product of age and experience.

It's your responsibility to properly direct his education. Socialization opportunities include taking him along with you on daily errands, visits to friends, and car trips. Vary the routine in order to introduce him to something or someone new each day. This should include mental challenges, different environments, other animals, and most important, a wide array of men, women, and children.

Poodle puppies are mentally resilient, but they are not immune to psychic trauma. When your puppy first arrives, try to maintain a calm environment. Poodles are very sensitive to their surroundings. A busy household need not be an emotionally charged, chaotic environment.

Poodles learn quickly, and your puppy can form accidental learned associations by observing your behavior. Make a conscious effort to communicate consistent ideas, and avoid sending the wrong messages through your expressions and gestures. For instance, a puppy can be intimidated by an exuberant reaction when he arrives in his new home. Even though everyone will be anxious to see him and make friends, this should be a low-key welcome. A puppy may interpret friendly demonstrations quite differently if someone stares into his face, talks to him in a loud, excited tone, or reaches down to grab him for a bear hug. Give him sufficient time to become accustomed

Breed Needs

Puppy Kindergarten

Puppy kindergarten is often considered a precursor to formal training. Although these classes are less structured, they are no less important. They can have a tremendous impact on your puppy's confidence and social development during his critical learning phase.

Puppies are introduced to basic obedience, but the classes' primary purpose is to provide positive social interaction with a variety of people and dogs. Sessions usually include some play time, but this should be limited and structured. Puppies should be learning to focus their attention and respond to humans, rather than getting the idea that it's fine to ignore you in favor of their playmates.

Interactive Play

Don't underestimate the value of interactive play as a form of training. It can facilitate bonding, trust, and communication. But it can also transmit inappropriate ideas about acceptable behavior with humans. Unless everyone reinforces rules about play times and play areas, your puppy will pester you for attention and demand to play whenever it suits him. If rough play is forbidden, this message must be consistently reinforced by every human he plays with. Barking, grabbing, jumping, and lunging may seem like innocent puppy behaviors, but condoning them sends a message that your Poodle will carry into adulthood. Dogs cultivate these habits for the simple reason that they work. Poodles are too smart to waste their energy repeating strategies that never result in a payoff.

to his new home and the mannerisms of everyone around him. This is especially important if your household includes young children, who may inadvertently intimidate a puppy while trying to make friends with him.

Consistency and Structure

Regardless of who is primarily responsible for the puppy's care, every person in the household will interact with him on some level. Therefore, everyone should be in agreement concerning major aspects of his care. Failing to agree on these points before his arrival will inevitably lead to friction between family members. It will also set the stage for behavior and training problems.

Implement a structured schedule so that your puppy has no insecurities about his daily needs. Begin with the basics. Every day he will need to eat, sleep, play, and eliminate. Depending on his age, his daily schedule should include one to three meals, four to eight potty breaks, grooming, and play sessions. Everyone in the household should have input when designing your puppy's daily care schedule. He is going to be a member of your family pack, and emergencies do arise. There will be times when another family member will be asked to fix his dinner or take him out for a walk.

Decide in advance if he will have regular daily walks, take his potty breaks in some part of your backyard, or in the case of Toys, be trained to use paper or a litter tray. Don't wait until he arrives before deciding if he will sleep in his crate or on your bed. Crate training will become quite difficult if the puppy is shuttled randomly from one to the other.

Everyone in the household must agree about boundaries and household rules for the puppy. For instance, you must plan how to supervise him in order to keep him out of mischief. Will he be restricted to certain areas of your home? Is he going to be allowed on the furniture? Poodle puppies are especially good at initiating play with anyone and everyone they meet. It will be impossible to discourage your puppy from roughhousing indoors if some family members encourage him to play in this manner.

Training Your Puppy

Is everyone in the household going to participate in the puppy's training? This can be wonderful or disastrous. Done properly, it will provide many more opportunities to reinforce desired behavior. On the other hand, if you all choose to implement your own rules and methods, the puppy will become hopelessly frustrated and confused. As a result, he may simply ignore you if he believes that his behavior is irrelevant to his success in your social pack. Worse yet, he may shut down and become passive, refusing to interact at all.

A structured training class is certainly beneficial, but in reality, it will account for a very small part of your puppy's education. Poodles constantly formulate new ideas from their experiences. Therefore, training must become part of your puppy's daily routine from the start. There are two ways of doing this. One option is to let your Poodle take charge of the process. Before you know it he will have you responding on command to prepare his food, take him for walks, dish out treats, and fluff his pillows. Your living room will be transformed into a doggy gym, with paw prints on the furniture and squeaky toys under the rug.

HOME BASICS
Teaching Your Puppy to Love Grooming

There is a difference between insulating your puppy from genuine dangers and indulging unwarranted reactions. Every puppy should learn to accept the idea of being picked up and held, even though some have an instinctive aversion to being restrained or closely examined. Puppies usually begin to exhibit this response around three or four months of age. A previously cooperative puppy may suddenly object to having his ears cleaned or nails clipped. This response must be addressed as soon as it occurs. A frantic, struggling puppy can be injured if accidentally dropped. More seriously, a dog who panics when handled or restrained will become impossible to groom or treat for medical conditions. Your Poodle's life will include a great deal of avoidable stress if you fail to impart this concept during his puppyhood.

From the day your puppy arrives, pick him up, cuddle him, and examine his feet, his ears, and his teeth. Reward him with praise and a treat whenever he responds cooperatively. If he begins to struggle or panic, do not reprimand him or forcibly restrain him. End the lesson, but repeat the routine daily until he is comfortable being handled. This is also the time to familiarize him with every aspect of grooming.

Grooming shops typically won't accept dogs that are not fully vaccinated, so plan to groom your puppy at home until he is at least four months old. Although he doesn't require much grooming at this age, these sessions provide valuable training. Reward him for standing quietly on a table while he is brushed. Lay him on his side while you brush his legs and belly. Introduce him to the noise and vibration of an electric clipper and blow dryer. Trim his nails, clean his ears, band his topknot, and go through the motions of cleaning his teeth at least once a week. This should become an enjoyable experience for both of you.

Or, you can do the training. This process can actually happen just as effortlessly. However, it does require a conscious effort to instill a cause-and-effect relationship between your puppy's behavior and his access to valued resources like attention, treats, and playtime. Implementing this type of program is far more effective than trying to revise longstanding bad habits or manage bad behavior with a constant string of ineffective reprimands.

For example, every owner enjoys watching his or her pet happily devour a meal. This does not mean that a good appetite should be accompanied by boorish manners. When you prepare your puppy's food, ask him to sit, and do not offer him the dish until he is polite and cooperative. This mini lesson teaches self-control and reinforces your household rules in a powerful way. Through his daily interactions with your family, he should learn what type of behavior is expected—and rewarded. Never give him a treat or toy without asking him to do something to earn it.

Of course, this is a two-way street. While guiding your puppy into your pack, you must remain vigilant to his responses. Remember, Poodles are both highly sensitive and extremely curious, and you must be attuned to your puppy's emotional state. Naturally, you want to minimize his exposure to distressing situations. In order to become a happy, confident adult he must learn that the world is a safe and friendly place. Puppies do experience phases when their fearful responses are intensified, but every dog develops differently, and these periods cannot be reliably predicted. It is impossible to plan a socialization schedule to accommodate this issue, but you should make every effort to ensure that his social encounters are positive. Observe his reactions and step in if he seems overly anxious or stressed. A more gradual introduction may be warranted in some situations, but puppies do bounce back from scary experiences. This is a part of life.

Housetraining

Owners are naturally anxious to get their puppy housetrained quickly. Whether you are training him to use paper or to eliminate during daily walks, the concept is the same. You must encourage him to relieve himself at a specific time and location, and discourage him from doing so at other times. Show him where and when he is supposed to relieve himself. Reinforce this by rewarding him when he gets it right. Don't complicate the situation by leaving him unsupervised.

SHOPPING LIST

Puppy Supplies

Nylon or leather collar.

Toy: 3/8 inch (1 cm) wide, 6–10 inches (15–25 cm) long

Mini: 1/2–3/4 inch (1.3–2 cm) wide, 10–14 inches (15–25 cm) long

Standard: 3/4–1 inch (2–2.5 cm) wide, 14–16 inches (35–40 cm) long

He should not be able to slip his head out of a properly fitting collar (or get his foot caught inside of it), but you should be able to slip a finger between the collar and his neck. Regularly adjust the fit as your puppy grows.

Harness. A nylon or leather step-in harness does not encircle the neck, but it must fit snugly around the chest for safety. To calculate size, add 2 inches (5 cm) to the measurement around the widest part of your puppy's chest, behind the elbows.

Toy: 3/8 inch (1 cm) wide

Mini: 5/8 inch (1.6 cm) wide

Standard: 1 inch (2.5 cm) wide

Leash. A nylon or leather, 5- to 6-foot lead is preferable to a retractable lead, which is too long to permit good control or safe supervision.

Toy: 1/8–3/8 inch (.3–1 cm) wide

Mini: 5/8 inch (1.6 cm) wide

Standard: 1 inch (2.5 cm) wide

Crate. To calculate crate size, measure your puppy's height from the paw to the top of his shoulders, and his body length from the point of his chest to the back of his thigh. Add 4 inches (10 cm) to each measurement. This allows your puppy ample room to stand up and turn around inside the crate. An overly large crate is not safe for travel and will not be useful for housetraining. Both wire and plastic crates can be used. Wire crates can be folded for storage, but they are not acceptable for air travel. Folding nylon mesh crates are not recommended for puppies.

Exercise Pens and Gates. A portable folding exercise pen will keep your puppy safe both indoors and outdoors. It should be made of stainless steel or coated with epoxy finish to prevent rusting. The wire should be narrowly spaced to prevent a puppy from getting his foot or jaw caught between the bars.

Recommended size for Toys and Minis: 36 inches (91 cm) high

Recommended size for Standard: 48 inches (122 cm) high

If your puppy is a climber, you may need a clip-on top panel for the pen.

Temporary Barriers: Models made with epoxy-coated wire mesh are preferable to wood or plastic mesh, which can be chewed.

Dishes. Dishes should be stainless steel or ceramic for easy cleaning and chewing prevention. Styles with higher sides help keep his ears clean.

Bedding. Bedding should be durable and washable. Good choices include heavy cotton and artificial sheepskin. Cushions should have removable covers and recessed zippers to prevent chewing.

Cleaning Supplies. Use natural products to remove stains, like a dilution of white vinegar and water or baking soda, rather than chemical disinfectants. Enzyme odor neutralizers are the best choice for cleaning up housetraining accidents.

Housetraining builds on a dog's natural inclination to keep his immediate surroundings clean. Puppies begin to do this as soon as they can walk. However, they vary in their ability to learn housetraining routines. This is partly physical. Puppies need to eliminate very frequently. Until three months of age, they may need to go every hour or two during the day, even though they learn to hold it through the night at a fairly young age. After three months, they develop better physical control but usually still need seven or eight potty breaks each day. By four months of age, five or six potty breaks should be adequate, and an adult should be comfortable with four daily potty breaks.

Puppies also differ in their ability to retain information, and they usually have occasional lapses before they are perfectly housetrained. Their learning curves may vary, but if you stick to the routine, housetraining will be successful. Commonly, owners prematurely assume that the puppy is trained and stop reinforcing the routine a bit too soon.

Provide a convenient, accessible area for your puppy to eliminate. Accompany him to his spot at scheduled intervals, and allow 10 or 15 minutes for him to get down to business. Stay with him until he relieves himself. Otherwise you will not know when has finished, and you will not be able to reward him immediately. For some puppies, it also helps to use a key phrase like *potty*. If he does nothing within a reasonable time, confine him to his crate for an hour, then repeat these steps until you have success.

As you spend time with your puppy, it becomes easier to predict when he needs to go, based on his body language. Typical signs include sudden sniffing and circling, or running off to a distant corner of the room. Quickly take him to his elimination spot and reward him when he gets it right. If you are vigilant, he will not have opportunities to have accidents in the house, which eventually evolve into poor housetraining habits.

If your puppy has an accident, punishment will not speed up his learning curve. Scrupulously clean the area with baking soda or enzyme odor neutralizer to remove odors, and review your training and supervision routine. If, despite your best efforts, he has repeated accidents, add more potty breaks to his schedule. If that fails, schedule a veterinary check to rule out underlying medical conditions such as a bladder infection or intestinal parasites.

Helpful Hints

Housetraining accessories, like belly bands for males and training pants for females, have become extremely popular in recent years. They are not meant to replace housetraining, however. They are a useful deterrent for dogs addicted to territorial marking.

Your puppy should be checked for internal parasites during his initial visit to the veterinarian. This simple test will detect most problems, but it is not infallible. The life cycle of these parasites can make them difficult to identify in stool samples, which can complicate the diagnosis. Puppies most often harbor roundworms, but hookworms, whipworms, tapeworms, coccidia, and giardia can also cause problems. If your puppy suffers repeated bouts of lethargy and diarrhea, continue testing even if the initial samples come up negative. All of these conditions are highly treatable and do not pose any serious health issue if detected and treated early. Parasite infestation is not always accompanied by outward symptoms, but it will interfere with your puppy's response to vaccinations and leave him susceptible to diseases he would normally fight off. Parasites can also cause complications like nutritional deficiencies and anemia.

Toy Poodles are often labeled as difficult to housetrain for reasons ranging from small bladders to poor concentration skills. These are excuses, not valid explanations. Owners of Toys tend to take housetraining and supervision less seriously, thus giving the puppy plenty of opportunities to have accidents and learn bad habits. After three or four repetitions, an elimination pattern starts to become instilled.

Crate Training

Crate training is a good idea for several reasons, and it is often recommended as an aid to housetraining, based on the fact that dogs have a natural aversion to soiling their den. Unless the crate is far too large, a puppy will do his best to avoid having an accident there. However, if he is confined for unreasonably long periods he will be forced to overcome his instinct for cleanliness. In that case, housetraining and crate training become far more difficult.

If you acquired your puppy from a breeder, he has probably been introduced to a crate for eating, sleeping or traveling. If not, begin familiarizing him with crate training as soon as he arrives. This also reinforces the concepts of remaining calm and spending time alone.

Start by creating a positive association with the crate. Place a favorite toy inside and allow him to investigate it as he pleases. When he goes in, immediately toss in a treat and praise him with a special phrase. After doing this for a couple of days, close the door and leave him for 10 or 15 minutes. If he begins to protest, ignore it. Whining, crying, barking, and digging in the crate are demands for attention. Giving in will send a clear message. Once he is quiet, even if it is just for two minutes, let him out. As he gets older, gradually increase his crate time. By three months, he should be able to remain crated for three or four hours. By four months, he should be able to make it through the night in his crate.

Puppy Toys

Don't go wild buying toys when your puppy first arrives. Start with a few, and slowly add to the collection as you learn his preferences. This also helps you get an idea of which toys are safe for him. Some puppies never leave a mark on their toys, while others are intent on chewing them to bits. Most Poodles love squeaky toys, but some puppies will tear them apart and try to eat the squeakers and stuffing. Soft rubber and plush toys won't work for them. Hard toys like cow hooves and sterilized bones may seem like a safer choice. But if your puppy is a dedicated chewer, these extremely hard materials may cause tooth damage. The fact that something is marketed as a dog toy does not imply that it meets any safety standards. Follow your breeder's recommendations and supervise your puppy during

play. In general, safe chew toys include hard rubber toys, knotted ropes, and nylon bones. Most breeders do not recommend dental chews because they can be a choking hazard. Choose toys that are appropriately sized for your Poodle. Never give him anything that fits entirely into his mouth. Supervise when giving him a new toy and take it away if it seems to pose any risk. Well-chewed favorites should also be replaced periodically for safety.

It's also helpful to rotate his toys. If they are all left out, he will become bored with them. A long-forgotten toy will elicit the same reaction as a brand-new one, and save you lots of money. Stowing them away between play sessions is good housekeeping, and it helps him to understand that play happens at certain times.

Choosing a Veterinarian

The simplest way to find a veterinarian is through recommendations from your puppy's breeder or dog-owning friends.

Here are a few points to consider:

- Is the practice within reasonable driving distance?
- Are the clinic hours compatible with your schedule?
- Can you book weekend or same-day appointments?
- Can you request appointments with the veterinarian of your choice?
- Does the clinic offer emergency care? Are hospitalized pets monitored overnight?

- Is the office staff personable and efficient?
- Are you allowed to visit areas where hospitalized pets are kept?
- What is the range of diagnostic services provided by the practice?
- Are any specialty or additional services—such as pet sitting, boarding, or grooming—offered?
- What payment options do they offer? If you have pet health insurance confirm that they accept your insurance plan.

Most important, do you feel confident about the veterinarian's interest in your puppy? Are you comfortable communicating with him or her? Does he or she willingly answer questions and respond to phone calls in a timely manner? You are ultimately responsible for your pet's health decisions. These may range from understanding the possible side effects of routine drugs or deciding how best to treat a major illness or injury. Toy owners should also keep in mind that veterinarians are not equally skilled at caring for small breeds. Understanding toy dogs' response to stress, anesthesia, vaccinations, and drug dosages is a major factor in their care.

Helpful Hints

Pet Insurance

Pet insurance is designed to work like health insurance to offset veterinary expenses.

It's more economical to sign up for pet insurance while your Poodle is a puppy, but read the fine print before choosing a plan. Premiums, deductibles, and coverage can vary tremendously. Some packages cover routine services like annual exams, vaccinations, heartworm preventative, and spay/neuter surgery. These usually have higher premiums. Others cover only major illness and injury. Many plans will not cover elective procedures, preexisting conditions, or late-onset disorders linked to hereditary defects.

Choosing a Groomer

If you plan to have your Poodle professionally groomed, he will be visiting his groomer every six to eight weeks. This person will play an important role in his life. Grooming should be a pleasant experience for your Poodle, not something he comes to dread. In addition to skill and artistic sense, look for someone who is knowledgeable about dog care and interested in your pet's well-being. A groomer may be the first to spot early clues of a health or behavior issue.

Here are a few questions to help you make a choice:

- What are the standard fees? Does this include extras like ear cleaning, nail clipping, bows, or nail polish?
- How far in advance must you book appointments?
- Does the groomer offer pickup and delivery, or extra services such as daycare or pet sitting?
- What type of soaps and conditioners are used?

FYI: Vaccine Components

Core Vaccines
- Distemper
- Parvovirus
- Adenovirus 2 (hepatitis)
- Rabies

Non-Core
- Leptospirosis
- Lyme disease
- Giardia

- Does the groomer use cage dryers? If so, are dogs monitored at all times?
- Are dogs restrained or tranquilized for grooming?
- Can you inspect the area where dogs are kept during appointments? Is it clean and secure?
- Is a veterinarian on call? Are staff members trained in pet first aid?

Professional groomers don't have to be licensed, but many have credentials from organizations like International Professional Groomers (IPG), the International Society of Canine Cosmetologists (ISCC), the National Dog Groomers Association of America (NDGAA), or the World Wide Pet Supply Association (WWPSA). Certified groomers are more likely to keep their skills up to par by attending conferences, seminars, and competitions.

Puppy Vaccinations

A puppy's vaccinations are usually administered as a series of combined shots known as the DHPP vaccine (distemper, hepatitis [adenovirus], parainfluenza, parvovirus). This combination may include from four to seven components. Your puppy may or may not need all of them, depending on his lifestyle and the prevalence of certain diseases in your area of the country. The vaccine components are classified as "core" (essential) and "non-core" (optional).

Annual rabies vaccination is legally required in every state. However, your puppy's breeder may recommend waiting until he is a certain age or size before receiving it. Most breeders advise against giving it in combination with the DHPP vaccination. Consult your puppy's breeder and veterinarian regarding the need for non-core vaccines.

Your puppy should receive his first DHPP vaccination at approximately eight weeks of age. By then, his natural maternal antibodies will have waned, leaving him with little or no protection against diseases like distemper and parvovirus. Vaccinations will not be effective until this maternal immunity has declined, so there is nothing to be gained by giving them too early. The first dose should be followed up by two more vaccinations, spaced at least three weeks apart. He should receive the final one at 16 weeks. By that age, 99 percent of puppies have lost all of the maternal protection that could interfere with earlier vaccinations.

Current vaccination protocols advise giving booster shots every three years rather than annually. A blood test to determine antibody titer level can confirm when additional shots are needed.

Breed Needs

Until your puppy is vaccinated, you must shield him from exposure to infection. However, these weeks also represent his critical learning period. Keeping him in isolation may be the best way to protect his health, but it will stunt his mental development. Strike a balance by providing varied social experiences while avoiding potential contact with other dogs. Safe alternatives include visiting friends, shopping errands, and car rides. Avoid public places frequented by dogs such as dog parks, doggy daycare centers, or grooming shops.

Teething

A puppy's 28 deciduous teeth will slowly be replaced by 42 permanent teeth around 16 weeks of age, but this is subject to variation. Small breeds often begin teething later than large breeds, females usually start teething earlier than male littermates, and summer puppies tend to start earlier than winter puppies.

Teething may take three to five months, and it can have a big impact on your puppy's behavior. He may seem withdrawn, tired, and cranky and have difficulty focusing on training because of the discomfort. Some puppies suffer quite a bit of mouth and jaw pain during these weeks, and it may be advisable to temporarily curtail leash training. Most often, puppies become fixated on chewing. This habit can be managed, but it cannot be prevented through behavior modification. Chewing will help to relieve his stress and speed up the teething process. Provide him with several safe chew toys and keep an eye on the table legs.

Retained Puppy Teeth

Ideally, each permanent tooth will erupt directly under the baby tooth it is destined to replace, gradually absorbing its root and pushing it out. Occasionally, the permanent tooth emerges slightly out of position. As a result, the puppy ends up with an extra retained tooth. This typically happens with the upper canines, less often with the lower canines.

If retained puppy teeth have not loosened by seven months, they should be extracted. This is a surgical procedure done under anesthesia. If they are left in place, they can cause crowding and push other teeth out of proper alignment. Retained puppy teeth are also prone to infection due to plaque buildup. They are fragile and can also fracture easily. A broken tooth will abscess, causing intense pain and infection, which can travel down the root canal to the jaw.

10 **Questions** on Puppy Proofing

 Are household toxins safely out of your puppy's reach? Puppies can be poisoned by a multitude of dangerous chemicals commonly found in the home, such as bleach, detergent, solvents, pesticides, herbicides, toilet bowl cleaner, dryer sheets, and furniture polish. Surprisingly, they are even more likely to be poisoned by ingesting prescription medications. Human and veterinary drugs, including vitamins, should be stored out of a puppy's reach.

Puppies can also be poisoned by licking household cleaners from surfaces, or off of their paws or coats, absorbing them topically, or breathing fumes.

 **Is your puppy protected from drowning hazards?** Although Poodles are water dogs, do not assume that your puppy can swim. Inexperienced puppies can drown as a result of panic or exhaustion, but most canine drowning deaths occur when the dog becomes trapped in water—for example, if a dog cannot climb out of a swimming pool, or falls through the ice of a partly frozen lake or pond. Less obvious hazards include cisterns, wells, hot tubs, fountains, and ornamental ponds. A small dog or a puppy can drown in a toilet, large bucket, or the water accumulated on top of a swimming pool

cover. Close toilet lids, empty wading pools between use, and never leave your puppy unattended near standing water.

 Is your puppy safe from burn injuries? Electrical cords and Christmas lights are familiar puppy dangers. Outlets can also be a potential electrocution hazard. Ideally, puppies should be restricted from rooms with accessible electrical cords. Chewing deterrents like bitter apple spray will discourage some puppies from chewing electrical cords. Don't assume that your puppy will instinctively avoid hot ovens, fireplaces, woodstoves, candles, and fire pits.

 Is your puppy protected from falls? Poodle puppies possess a dangerous combination of athleticism and curiosity. In consequence, they can fall into window wells, down stairs, out of windows, into holes, and off of furniture. The result can be broken bones, spinal injuries, or head trauma. Install baby gates or safety netting to prevent falls from staircases, decks, hallways, and balconies. Windows should be kept closed or covered with screens. Puppies can also be injured climbing or jumping onto chairs or shelf units. Leaving tempting items on counters or tabletops will also encourage these stunts.

5 **Is your puppy safe from choking dangers?** Puppies explore their world by tasting. This oral fixation is even more highly developed in retrieving breeds like Poodles. Remind visitors to keep an eye on their personal items. A curious puppy will not hesitate to pilfer small toys, medications, and cosmetics from pockets and purses of guests. Trash receptacles are a ubiquitous trouble zone—spoiled food, bones, tinfoil, steel wool, and corn cobs can cause poisoning or intestinal obstruction. The best remedy is stowing trash in an inaccessible location and taking it out frequently.

6 **Is your home escape-proof?** As soon as your puppy arrives, begin teaching him to come when called. Keep in mind, however, that puppies are impulsive. An open door or gate can be an invitation to investigate the neighborhood and confront dangers ranging from dog thieves to speeding cars.

His home turf should be limited to areas that are securely gated. Self-closing gates with security latches add an extra level of safety. Always confine or crate him if gates and doors are likely to be left open because of visitors or workmen in your house.

7 **Is your puppy safe from collisions with humans?** Quite a few accidents happen when a hurried, distracted person trips over a puppy, seriously injuring both parties. It's easier to remain aware of your puppy's whereabouts if he is restricted to specific rooms of the house. He should be safely out of the vicinity whenever you are preoccupied with complicated tasks like home repairs or cooking.

8 **Is your puppy safe from risky encounters with other pets?** Large, aggressive dogs and wildlife are obvious dangers. Less obvious hazards are easy to overlook. Puppies can be drowned in aquariums, bitten by large birds, and scratched by cats. Never assume that other pets will readily befriend a new puppy. Even a friendly dog can accidentally injure a puppy during rough play. Have a system in place to keep your pets separated when you are unable to supervise.

9 **Is your puppy safe in your backyard?** If your puppy can fit his head through a gap in the fence, he will be able to squeeze his body through, too. He may also try to squeeze into crawl spaces under the house or porch, or through fencing around a deck or swimming pool. Fertilizers, compost piles, swimming pool treatment chemicals, and snail and slug bait should be stored out of reach. Toxic garden plants like grapevines, azalea, castor bean, sago palm, honeysuckle, lilies, oleander, and yew should be fenced off. Never apply pesticides, fertilizers, or herbicides in areas where your puppy plays. If it's impossible to puppy proof your entire yard, purchase or build a dog run.

10 **Is your puppy safe from auto hazards?** Part of your puppy's socialization should include learning to ride in his crate during car trips. This is the canine equivalent of wearing a seatbelt. When he exits the car, always attach his leash before opening the door. And always know your puppy's whereabouts before driving a vehicle on or off of your property.

Chapter Five

Living with a Poodle

When you decided to get a dog, you made the choice to devote your extra time, energy, and money to a very demanding venture. Dogs need many things, but the most important ingredient is your personal attention. They also require patience. This is especially true for puppies, but even adult Poodles have their moments of misbehavior. You will also face countless routine tasks that come with owning a pet. You may have envisioned romping with your Poodle in a sunny meadow, but there is plenty of mundane grooming, walking, and housework that come along with that idyllic picture.

The Responsibilities of Poodle Ownership

Your next set of responsibilities materialized when you signed the sales contract for your Poodle. This included guarantees regarding the dog's health and quality. It also outlined your responsibilities regarding his care. If you have family members or housemates, your decision to acquire a dog also included responsibilities to them, such as training your Poodle to be a well-adjusted family member who is enjoyable to have around.

You also have responsibilities to the outside world. Your Poodle will quickly be labeled a neighborhood nuisance if he is permitted to bark constantly, escape from your yard, or harass passersby. Poodle ownership also entails a responsibility to know your local laws regarding dog ownership. Most towns and cities require dogs to be leashed whenever they are in public. Many have ordinances requiring owners to pick up after their dogs. Every state requires that dogs be immunized against rabies. Your town may also require annual dog licensing. If your dog is picked up by the dog warden, a license will ensure that he is returned to you. Unlicensed dogs are impounded, and you will face fees and penalties.

All of these things add up to a lot of responsibility. Is it worth it? Mounting scientific evidence confirms the value of dog ownership and has led to the creation of therapy dog and prison dog programs. Prison dog programs help the inmates learn tolerance, empathy, responsibility, and job skills training, including grooming dogs. Therapy dog programs bring dogs into hospitals, rehab centers, and hospices to provide companionship and emotional support for patients. These structured programs are designed to provide emotional and physical benefits that dog lovers have long recognized. For example:

- Petting a dog lowers heart and blood pressure rates.
- Canine companionship offsets depression and loneliness, which enhances immune function.
- Caring for a dog provides mental and physical motivation to speed recovery from illness.

Your Poodle's Daily Routine

Dogs thrive on a consistent routine. It provides them with a sense of security and control over their environment. Poodles quickly learn to anticipate each part of their daily schedule, and this may occasionally drive you crazy. Your dog will remind you if you are five minutes late with the most mundane aspects of his schedule. Make things easy for both of you by designing a routine that fits seamlessly into your lifestyle.

Certain tasks must be incorporated into your schedule. For instance, puppies must be fed three times a day, and adults twice. Free feeding is more convenient, but it is not recommended for Poodles. You must dedicate daily time to his grooming needs. Whether he is a puppy or adult, you must devote time to reinforcing his housetraining routine until he learns it. Even after he is reliably trained, you must ensure that he visits his potty area at scheduled times to prevent housetraining mishaps. He also needs daily play, exercise, and social interaction with his family.

CHECKLIST

Responsibilities

- ✔ Train and socialize your Poodle.
- ✔ Make sure he has a collar tag, microchip, or tattoo, and a license if required.
- ✔ Keep him leashed in public, and have a poop scoop or plastic bag handy.
- ✔ Keep his health checks, deworming, and vaccinations up to date.
- ✔ Provide him with adequate training, exercise, and social interaction.
- ✔ Keep him clean, tidy, and free from external parasites.

Strategies to Prevent Common Training and Behavior Problems

Despite the best intentions, some owners shortchange crucial canine requirements because they find it difficult to combine them with the demands of daily life. Foremost among these are training, socialization, and exercise. It is no coincidence that most canine behavior problems result from neglecting one or more of these needs.

It's easier to incorporate these needs into your normal routine, than to struggle to meet unrealistic goals, like heading off for training classes after work or getting up an hour early to jog with your dog every morning. In reality, there is a good chance that your Poodle will get bored with a rigid schedule before you do. The ideal Poodle routine should be both structured and unstructured, which seems contradictory at first but actually makes a lot of sense.

Your Poodle needs ongoing reinforcement and encouragement from you in order to learn your household rules. At the same time, he needs variety and challenges. This dilemma is a product of our modern lifestyle. For most of the breed's history, Poodles functioned as working dogs. Their care and training was inseparable from their owner's daily routine. A seventeenth-century working Poodle accompanied his owner throughout the day, performing a wide range of tasks when requested. Needless to say, our lifestyles have changed over the centuries. You won't, for instance, expect your Poodle to retrieve ducks from your swimming pool. However, this breed remains mentally geared to function as a working partner, responding to the unpredictable situations that characterized waterfowl hunting.

Poodles proved to be awesome students long before formal dog training was invented. Without the benefit of structured lessons, working Poodles achieved an incredibly high level of precision and teamwork.

It may seem unorthodox, but you can implement a similar arrangement to effortlessly train your Poodle. Brief lessons throughout the day will appeal to him much more than repetitious drills. These regular mental challenges will ultimately produce the level of teamwork that was expected from a working Poodle. For instance, a working Poodle had to be attentive in order to mark the location of game and retrieve it. Very often, he would willingly perform a blind retrieve, following his partner's hand signals and voice commands to search for game that was out of his sight range.

Keep a few treats, and possibly a clicker, in your pocket, and use them to reinforce basic commands throughout the day. You can integrate short lessons into every type of activity. Ask your Poodle to heel while you take out the trash, fetch a toy while you make a phone call, or sit and stay while you check your e-mail. This will improve his focus and responsiveness as he learns to anticipate requests from you. Even if he is well trained, these exercises keep his skills sharpened without taking time from your schedule for training classes. When he has mastered one skill, build on it to teach something more complex.

In addition to basic commands, this method will help your Poodle learn self-control and patience. Poodles have an undeserved reputation for being rambunctious, simply because their owners have not taught them self-control. It was essential for a working Poodle to remain calm and quiet until sent to retrieve. Noisy, wild behavior could spook the birds, capsize a boat, or cause a gun to accidentally misfire. If your Poodle has difficulty focusing his attention, ask him to settle down for five-minute breaks through the course of the day.

During these breaks, say his name in a soft, soothing tone, and insist that he remain calmly at your side. Hold his head in your hands, stroke his ears, run your hands down his neck, sides, and legs, and rub his chest, belly, and tail. Praise him for remaining quiet. This little break reinforces your bond, encourages calmness, and provides an opportunity to give your dog a quick daily health check. After five minutes, praise him with a special phrase to signal that he is free to go. Eventually, extend the length of his breaks, asking him to sit quietly as you work at your desk or watch TV. Once you have instilled this concept, he will happily chill out when asked, which is far more effective than threatening or intimidating an overexcited dog into remaining quiet.

It's even more important for him to learn to settle down when he is keyed up. Hunting is characterized by tedium interrupted with sudden intense activity. A working Poodle needed to switch modes on command. Occasionally, call your Poodle during playtime and ask him to sit. With practice, it will become progressively easier for him to switch modes and settle down. This is an extremely useful skill that will prove valuable in a myriad of situations.

A working Poodle had to be trusted to carry game in his mouth without biting into it, or worse yet, deciding to abscond with dinner. Dogs that chewed a bird or refused to give it up were considered "hard-mouthed" and simply did not make the grade. Today, this exercise is known as *retrieve to hand*. After retrieving game, the dog is expected to hold it softly but firmly and to release it on command. A relaxed, cooperative dog takes treats gently and slowly and relinquishes items without a fuss. For retrievers, this is known as having a soft mouth.

Your Poodle should willingly allow you to take anything from him. This response is the product of mutual trust and recognition that you are his pack leader. A confrontational approach is guaranteed to undermine trust and put him on the defensive. Your goal is voluntary cooperation. You must be firm, consistent, and fair. Always ask first, do not take no for an answer, and reward his cooperation.

When your Poodle is happily playing with a toy, call his name, make eye contact, and ask him to give you the item. Offer a food reward in exchange or put your hand on the item he is holding while offering something better in its place. When offering your Poodle a treat, insist on good manners. Never hand over the goods if he jumps, lunges, or nips your fingers. Nor should he be permitted to growl and snarl if you approach his dish. At the first sign of this behavior, begin counter-conditioning. Pick up the dish and hand-feed him several pieces of food. Praise him for taking them gently. This reinforces the idea that you are in charge of his food, and it is far easier than revising possessive aggression later on. This is especially important if you have children who may wander near the dog during mealtime, a very common situation for dog bites to occur.

Preempt Bad Habits

A working Poodle was at his master's side throughout the day. Unwanted behaviors were simply interrupted and redirected before they could blossom into habits. This close partnership also made it easy for a hunter to perceive his dog's intention. Poodles are often described as mind readers, but good Poodle owners have the same skill. Seventeenth-century subsistence hunters loved and respected their dogs. However, when they got home, cold, wet, tired, and hungry, it is unlikely that they had the time or energy to cope with problematic canine behavior. Every interaction with your Poodle is an opportunity to reinforce good behavior and rein in undesirable habits.

This is especially important when it comes to attention-seeking behaviors like barking, whining, pawing, jumping, nipping, and following your every move around the house. Responding to these antics in either a positive or negative fashion gives him the green light to continue. Ignore his demands, but don't ignore the dog. Simply redirect him to an activity of your choosing.

Breed Needs

There will be times when outdoor exercise is not an option. For Toy Poodles, a good run around the house can provide an excellent workout. For Minis and Standards, tricks or games like fetch and tug-o-war burn calories, strengthen muscles, and provide an aerobic workout. For example, the classic Poodle trick, sitting up on command, is great for promoting abdominal and back strength.

Daily Exercise

In addition to learning to be calm and well mannered, it's important to teach your Poodle to enjoy physical activity. These days, we make a commitment to exercise by joining a gym, but this also requires habit formation. Just like humans, dogs can and do become lazy and unmotivated. Unfortunately, for many dogs, the only meaningful activity they share with their owner centers around mealtime. This daily attention becomes just as rewarding as the food. The end result is an obese dog who is fixated on mealtime as his only source of positive daily interaction.

The demands of water retrieving fostered hardiness, stamina, and muscle tone. This work was demanding, but it was also structured. Dogs were not permitted to simply run wild and ignore the rules. This was not only a pointless waste of energy, it could spoil a day's hunt. Your Poodle should have two daily outings for brisk walking, off-lead running, or interactive play. Each of these sessions should run at least 15 minutes for Toys; 15 to 30 minutes for Miniatures; and 45 minutes for Standards.

Physical activity improves muscle tone, bone density, and cardiovascular function. Your Poodle will be happier, more alert, and content. Long walks are not only great exercise for both of you; they provide wonderful opportunities for your Poodle to investigate his environment, an extremely satisfying form of mental stimulation.

FYI: Does Your Poodle Need a Fenced Yard?

Owners often assume that a large, fenced yard solves the problem of providing exercise for a Poodle. He may happily run and play for a few minutes, but in short order he will notice that his partner is not on the scene. Many breeds are genetically programmed to work independently. They willingly guard flocks and stalk vermin without the aid of coworkers or companions. Poodles don't operate this way. They need interaction as an incentive to exercise. Your participation ensures that your Poodle forms good exercise habits and learns well-mannered play behavior. It's certainly easier to open the door and send him out, but interactive play provides limitless opportunities to build a rapport and reinforce training.

If you plan to exercise your Poodle in your yard, it must be securely fenced. He may be well behaved, but don't assume that he will never stray from your yard. Trained dogs regularly disappear from backyards for a variety of reasons. Four-foot fencing is adequate for Toy Poodles, and six-foot fencing is advisable for Miniatures and Standards. Electronic or invisible fencing is a popular alternative for many owners. It's less expensive than barrier fencing, which some communities prohibit. Dogs wear a collar that transmits an electric shock when they cross the underground fence perimeter. It does have drawbacks, however. If sufficiently frightened or excited, many dogs will disregard the shock and charge through the fence. Once outside, the collar may discourage them from returning home. It also provides no protection against other animals or potential dog thieves who may come onto your property.

Training Classes

For novice owners, classes can be an especially helpful way to learn basic principles of dog behavior and to identify budding behavior problems. For instance, inexperienced owners may overlook early signs of protective aggression, as this is not considered a typical Poodle trait.

Poodles have a well-developed instinct to protect their territory, and they can become quite tough and aggressive. Most Poodle lovers have read *Travels with Charley*, John Steinbeck's saga of traveling America with his beloved Poodle, Charley. One of the most memorable episodes of the book describes Steinbeck's shock when the normally meek Charley springs into action to defend his master against a charging bear. The lesson? Looks can be deceiving. Inside of every Poodle, there is a courageous watchdog ready to protect his pack. This natural instinct must be directed through training.

A skilled trainer can also provide advice on human-canine communication. Dogs have an innate ability to read human signals, a skill they learned over centuries of evolving alongside our species. For any social group to function, it's imperative to recognize the emotions and intent of our fellow pack members.

Socialization

A dog's social skills will be forgotten unless they are regularly used. Socialization should include regular contact with both dogs and people. Most owners are aware of the importance of socializing puppies during their optimum learning period, at 7–16 weeks. During these weeks puppies easily bond with unfamiliar individuals. Although this socialization period is finite, your Poodle's need to refine his social skills is ongoing. The fact that he enjoys meeting people doesn't mean that he will demonstrate appropriate behavior. Practice makes perfect. Poorly socialized dogs are usually thought of as timid, but in reality, the high stress of social situations can trigger a spectrum of unsuitable reactions. For instance, a socially insecure dog may turn into a bully. He may also become an overbearing bore, persistently seeking attention and approval from everyone he meets.

Poodles thrive on new experiences. Your dog's social calendar should include new people and unfamiliar places as well as his old favorites. Training classes and daycare programs can provide excellent opportunities to expand his social life.

Doggy Daycare

Growing numbers of busy owners utilize doggy daycare to ensure that their pets receive exercise, attention, and canine interaction. Dogs are dropped off at a daycare facility with competent professionals who supervise their care and activities for the day. In theory, this seems like an ideal arrangement. It's a great way to socialize a timid dog, provide company for a lonely dog, or ensure that an energetic dog gets plenty of activity.

Because daycare has become so popular, a range of programs is available in most cities. Some are secondary businesses run by veterinarians, boarding kennels, grooming salons, or training schools, and others are operated by individuals who may have limited experience and qualifications. Since these businesses are not monitored or licensed, you must do your own research to choose the right one for your Poodle.

Daycare programs routinely ban dogs with obvious aggression problems. However, there is potential for trouble whenever unfamiliar dogs interact. Daily exposure to a chaotic group of dogs can worsen behavior issues or create new ones. A poorly trained dog may forget everything he has learned. A rambunctious adolescent may evolve into an incorrigible delinquent. Without encouragement to socialize, a timid dog may become even more withdrawn. Well-housetrained dogs will develop bad habits if permitted to eliminate as they please rather than having scheduled potty breaks. Poodles are very sensitive to their environment, and a daycare program must provide more than a secure enclosure filled with a few dog toys and a human.

Every experience will have an impact on your dog's temperament. Choose a daycare routine that provides structure and positive, gentle training. Talk to several dog owners about their experiences with various local daycare programs. And ask for recommendations. Visit the facility to observe the level of supervision and staff skills. The premises should be clean and secure. Dogs should be kept in compatible groups of no more than 12–15 dogs per person. Staff members should provide ongoing interaction and individual time for each dog, rather than simply observing them through a fence or window. Along with a working knowledge of canine behavior, they should be trained in health basics as well as emergency procedures.

Poodles and Other Pets

A Poodle's social identity develops through a multifaceted process of ongoing interactions. This usually incorporates plenty of contact with humans and other dogs, but it may not include regular interaction with other species. A dog chasing a cat is a classic cartoon image. Unfortunately, this stereotype has instilled the belief that this is an inevitable canine response.

Although they may never become devoted companions, Poodles can learn to live peacefully with many other species. This is accomplished most easily if the introduction happens during a puppy's socialization period. Puppies can readily form bonds with any species during these weeks. However, that does not preclude the possibility of training an older dog to view cats, rabbits, and birds as part of the pack rather than as prey. This requires ongoing supervised encounters while you modify the behavior of both pets. For instance, even the sight of a Toy Poodle may trigger a flight response in a tiny ferret. If the ferret runs, the dog will instinctively chase. This experience reinforces the behavior you are seeking to discourage in both animals. Your goal is to prevent opportunities for these experiences to occur.

Through daily supervised contact you can systematically discourage your Poodle's desire to chase or hunt a smaller pet. Place the animals together in a small area where you can easily intervene. Interrupt the dog if he shows interest in stalking, and reward him for tolerating or ignoring the ferret. At the same time, the ferret will become accustomed to the dog's proximity and learn that he poses no threat. They both will have opportunities to learn each other's body language and gestures, which often vary a great deal between species. This process requires many weeks of daily behavior modification, and the animals should never be left together at other times. If you don't have the time to devote to this process, the best option is to keep the pets separated at all times.

Helpful Hints

Effective training and a structured routine are essential for multiple-dog homes. Choosing the right dog will also minimize problems. Ideally, the second dog should be another Poodle, but if you plan to acquire another breed, it should be comparable in size and temperament, but a different age and sex. Most altercations involve two young adults of the same sex. Neutered dogs are no less likely to engage in this behavior. Choose a puppy that willingly takes a subordinate role rather than the most dominant, outgoing one in the litter.

Multiple-Dog Homes

Poodles are such a pleasure to live with that many owners opt to add a second dog to their household. Poodles are sociable, tolerant of other dogs, and usually relish a canine playmate. Of course, you must also evaluate your ability to cope with extra expenses and time demands. This will entail more housecleaning, dog food, and veterinary care. More important, multiple dogs will quickly magnify any deficiencies in your canine manage-

ment skills. If your first dog is overweight and out of shape, it is unlikely that you will suddenly find more time to monitor canine fitness and nutrition. If your first dog is not well trained, the new dog will learn his bad habits, and you will cope with a double dose of misbehavior. If your first dog doesn't defer to you, adding a second one to your pack will provide more distractions. Dogs within a pack play off of each other and lose focus more easily. A trigger like a doorbell or stray cat can result in complete chaos if pack mentality overtakes them.

Your first dog may initially ignore the newcomer, which is a normal canine reaction. Accept this attitude; it will change in time. Allow the dogs to become friends at their own pace, which may require several weeks. Insist on polite, tolerant behavior from both, but never insist that they share food, territory, or possessions.

Adhere to the usual routine. For instance, if your first dog loves his daily walks, don't immediately include Junior. Each dog should have personal attention daily while they gradually adapt to each other. Use this time to give your first dog a refresher course in basic obedience. Teach Junior to respond to the same signals and commands to minimize confusion, and get yourself into the habit of prefacing every command with the appropriate dog's name. If necessary, do some housekeeping to ensure that toys, food, and other items likely to trigger possessive behavior are carefully controlled. Even if the dogs seem to get along, implement some arrangement to keep them separated when they are unsupervised.

A fight between dogs in a household is shocking, mainly because it seems to erupt without warning. That can happen, but it is extremely rare. Much more often, fighting is the culmination of subtle escalating conflict over food, territory, or attention. This is why it is important to control these resources in multiple-dog situations. This not only heads off most fights, it is critical to implementing and maintaining your role as pack leader.

Be on the lookout for subtle aggressive canine signals. If minor incidents are overlooked or ignored by the pack leader, the dogs will interpret this as a green light to take things a step further.

Common triggers include bringing a new dog into the household, especially an energetic puppy that tries the patience of an adult dog. Rivalry can also begin when a maturing puppy begins asserting authority, or a dominant dog loses his status due to age or illness. A new person in the household can also upset the status quo. If you are attentive, you will pick up on this canine feedback before it leads to growling or snarling. Permitting aggression to escalate into a fight sends the message that you are not in charge of the situation. Halt the encounter immediately, calmly, and firmly. Never resort to bullying or punishment. Poodles are highly sensitive to correction. Adding more stress to the situation will only fuel their anxiety. Crate each dog for a time-out, and arrange to keep them separated temporarily. Confiscate any resources responsible for triggering the fight. Add additional supervision and structure to their routine, and do not hesitate to consult a behaviorist if you feel unable to manage the situation.

Children and Poodles

Many studies have shown that children benefit from having a dog. The interaction improves a child's social skills, tolerance, self-confidence, and nonverbal communication. Learning to empathize with a dog also has an indirect impact on a child's sense of responsibility.

Children take their cues from parents regarding the dog's role in the family. Parents must be prepared to take a direct role in teaching children how to interpret the dog's body language and to treat the dog respectfully. If the dog is respected and well cared for, these values will be passed along to the next generation. The reverse is also true.

A Poodle can make an ideal child's companion as long as parents are committed to making this relationship work. It's an adult's job to recognize and prevent potential problems. If the dog gets hurt or the child is bitten, this is a failure of adult supervision. Children cannot be expected to exercise mature judgment or accurately interpret a dog's signals, but adults can provide clear ground rules.

Children should understand that it is never okay to run up and surprise the dog, or to make loud noises or sudden jerky movements when approaching the dog. A child may see this as a game, but the dog can view it as a threatening gesture. Encourage children to call the dog's name before approaching, especially when the dog is sleeping. The dog should have a place to retreat that is off-limits to children. When interacting with the dog, they should move calmly and deliberately, speak quietly, and touch the dog gently. Teasing, smacking, or hair pulling should never be tolerated. Any form of relentless teasing or rough treatment can provoke a dog to bite, but most incidents are food related. The safest approach is to not permit children to feed the dog. Needless to say, simply telling a child to follow these rules is not enough. You must supervise. At times when you cannot, the dog should be crated.

CAUTION

It is never a good idea to acquire any pet simply to teach a child responsibility. Children naturally want to help care for a dog, but these chores should be assigned based on the child's age and maturity. Asking a 50-pound child to walk a 75-pound dog is an invitation for disaster.

You should also train your Poodle to cope with children. Most important, train the dog to tolerate plenty of touching. Reward his forbearance with treats and praise. Even when they are trying their best to be gentle, children can become over-enthusiastic about rubbing and fondling a dog. Children should not be encouraged to feed the dog, but this can be difficult to prevent completely, so it is important to discourage any aggressive food-related behaviors like growling and food guarding. Your dog must also learn to politely accept a morsel of food without lunging or nipping.

If your children are over age seven, they should be encouraged to participate in the dog's basic training. This teaches the dog to defer to the child, and provides the child with better canine communication skills.

Communicating with Your Poodle

Voice Your Poodle listens to your voice constantly, and he tries to put these signals into context. Precede phrases with his name to emphasize that your words are meant for him. Be mindful of your tone. Dogs instinctively interpret low-pitched sounds as potentially aggressive. Higher tones sound submissive and vulnerable, like a puppy. In most situations a moderate tone works best. Your Poodle will interpret this as calming, reassuring, and neutral. Avoid constantly repeating commands. Say his name to get his attention, give the command once, and make sure that he follows through. Dogs are less likely to heed repetitive commands. From a canine perspective, this is akin to an outburst of mindless barking.

Also be aware of the duration of your words and phrases. Quick, clipped phrases imply excitement, which is useful for encouraging a reluctant dog to come. A long *nooo* can effectively stop a mischievous Poodle before he completes his crime.

The average dog comprehends approximately 60 distinct words and phrases. Intelligent dogs like Poodles can often discriminate up to 200. Your Poodle will learn many words through intentional training. Few Poodle owners teach their dogs to respond to *car keys* or *ice cream*. Nonetheless, Poodles clearly understand these terms.

Hands When Poodles want attention, they often focus on the hands, nudging and licking them as if they have a life of their own. You don't need to train your Poodle to be observant of your hands, but you must learn to consistently employ distinctive gestures when communicating with him. Hand gestures can be substituted for vocal commands, used to clarify them, or added to help your dog distinguish between closely related phrases. For instance, a quick directional cue of one or two fingers might signal that it's time to go in the door. Pointing in another direction could tell your Poodle it's time to go out the door and into the car. Your Poodle is adept at reading subtle gestures. If they are clear, consistent, and unique, there is no limit to the number of hand signals that your Poodle can learn.

Facial Expressions Dogs begin learning the importance of facial expressions as soon as their eyes open at three weeks of age. By the time a puppy transitions to his human family, he has a clear grasp of the intentions conveyed by many facial expressions. Unfortunately, expressions vary between species. Your Poodle is quite capable of learning to read your face, but be prepared to meet him halfway until you get onto the same wavelength.

Owners often fixate on voice commands, failing to realize that Poodles have been selectively bred to respond to a large range of social signals. Very often, your Poodle will look up to read your face if he is uncertain about what you want. Be mindful of what you convey. Tension or anxiety is often manifested unconsciously. A Poodle is too smart to buy the message if your voice says *good boy* while your face says something menacing.

Body Movement

Your Poodle will instinctively read, analyze, and remember the slightest nuances in your body language to gauge your emotional state. He is going to know when you are feeling friendly, worried, uncertain, or angry and will respond accordingly. It pays to be aware of this and maintain a calm, authoritative demeanor when interacting with him.

Your body language can be used to inhibit or encourage particular behaviors. Depending on whether you are a human or a dog, approaching quickly and abruptly or leaning over with a big sweeping gesture can be interpreted as either scary or welcoming. This doesn't mean that your Poodle should never be treated to spontaneous gestures. However, this informality will not be appreciated until you achieve trust and communication. Until then, read your dog's signals and be prepared to add extra cues if he seems confused about your intention. Also be aware that if your Poodle does not respond to training when you are tense or distracted, it is likely that something in your body language is sending a negative message.

Scents

Olfactory communication is the dog's primary means of comprehending his environment. In this respect, your Poodle will always have the upper hand. For instance, Poodles respond to scent cues in their environment, and they are quick to sound the alarm if they perceive a threat. You may not notice the mouse under the dresser, but don't dismiss your Poodle if he tells you to check it out.

Because scent is the dog's most acute sense, the canine brain is programmed to prioritize olfactory memories. The ability to process this cascade of information varies according to each dog's sensory abilities and emotional thresholds. In other words, every dog experiences the world in a slightly different way.

A dog's olfactory orientation is comparable to the human sense of vision. Your Poodle's most important information is filed away under smells rather than pictures. He is going to notice and respond to cues that you cannot detect, such as the complex chemical messages of pheromones. Although this is a species-specific communication system, dogs have no trouble reading human pheromones. Your Poodle will know if you are anxious, angry, or ill and respond accordingly.

Chapter Six

Health and Nutrition

T op-quality food is an obvious component of your pet's health. It's undeniably satisfying to watch a beloved dog happily devouring his food. However, ensuring optimum nutrition for your Poodle can get a bit complicated. The big issues are choosing the right foods and offering them in the proper amount. Never assume that your Poodle will stop eating when he feels full. Evolution has designed the dog to gorge when food is available and to endure long periods of deprivation. This was an excellent survival mechanism in ancient times, when dogs really did endure long fasts between each successful hunt. For house pets, it almost guarantees that they will become overweight without portion control.

Feeding Guidelines

Free feeding, or leaving food available at all times, is an invitation to over-eat. Puppies up to six months of age should be fed three measured portions of food each day. Portion size should be gradually decreased to compensate for declining energy requirements as a puppy's growth rate slows. When he reaches 40 percent of his adult weight, his daily ration should be approximately 1.5 times an adult-sized portion. When he reaches 80 percent of his adult weight, it should be reduced to 1.2 times the adult portion. After six months of age, his daily ration should be cut back from three to two meals per day.

Also keep in mind that every dog is different. Daily calorie requirements vary depending on factors such as age, physical condition, activity level, coat quality, climate, and temperament. However, the caloric needs of a typical inactive house pet are rather low. On average, one 8-ounce cup of kibble contains 390 calories. One 13.2-ounce can of food contains 400 calories.

A 5-pound Toy may start gaining weight if he regularly consumes more than 130 calories per day, so 1/3 of a cup or can of food should be enough. Add a few 40-calorie dog biscuits and some table scraps to this daily fare, and weight gain is inevitable. Owners are traditionally advised not to feed table scraps. However, foods like lean meat, chicken, and fresh vegetables can be a healthy addition to your Poodle's diet. It's fine to reward your

FYI: Calorie Requirements

10-pound (4.5-kg) dog: 218 calories per day	40-pound (18-kg) dog: 616 calories per day
15-pound (6.8-kg) dog: 295 calories per day	50-pound (22.6-kg) dog: 729 calories per day
20-pound (9-kg) dog: 366 calories per day	60-pound (27-kg) dog: 835 calories per day
30-pound (13.6-kg) dog: 497 calories per day	70-pound (31.7-kg) dog: 938 calories per day

Poodle with occasional treats and snacks as long as you subtract these calories from his daily total.

Also keep in mind that most premium dog foods contain more fat and calories than regular foods. If he eats one of these brands, your Poodle may need even smaller portions to meet his daily nutritional needs. Portion size should be based on his energy needs and body condition, rather than the typically generous recommendations on the package.

Forbidden Foods

We eat many foods knowing that they are not good for us, but there is no reason to share things like candy and pizza with your Poodle. These are not only empty calories; they may trigger needless digestive upsets.

Foods to avoid include:

- Pits and seeds of apples, cherries, peaches, and other fruits. These contain cyanide, which is poisonous to dogs as well as humans. Grapes and raisins can also be toxic to some dogs.
- Bones that create a risk of choking or intestinal obstruction
- Chocolate. Baker's chocolate poses the highest risk since it is more concentrated.
- Coffee grounds, tea and tea bags, and foods and drinks containing caffeine
- Macadamia nuts. These can cause weakness, muscle tremors, and paralysis.
- Nutmeg. The spice can cause seizures tremors and death.
- Onions
- Extremely salty, fatty, or spicy foods
- Alcoholic drinks

Nutrition

A dog can survive weeks without eating, but he will die within days without water. Water is the most important nutritional element of his diet, and fresh, clean water should always be available. If you are concerned about the quality of your tap water, consider investing in a water filter, which is far cheaper and more eco-friendly than bottled water.

Dogs are omnivorous, meaning they can derive required nutrients from a variety of sources. This has been a key to their success as a species. However, a balanced canine diet must include 20 different amino acids in precise ratios. Some can be synthesized by the body, but essential amino acids cannot be synthesized in sufficient quantities. They must be supplied by high-quality proteins like beef, chicken, and eggs. Prolonged deficiency of any essential amino acids will severely compromise health.

These essential amino acids are more likely to be found in commercial foods containing higher percentages of meat and lower ratios of carbohydrates and artificial ingredients. The ingredients of pet foods are listed in descending order based on the relative percentage of each one in the formula. Carbohydrates are good energy sources, but they should not be the primary ingredients of your Poodle's diet. Carbohydrate-based diets are more likely to lack one or more essential amino acids. Dogs must consume much larger quantities of these diets because the canine digestive system was not designed to efficiently extract nutrients from these sources.

The proteins in commercial formulas should be clearly identified on the label. Ambiguous terms like *flavoring* or *byproducts* should raise suspicion regarding the source or quality of the ingredients. Avoid foods containing artificial colors, flavors, or fillers. These are added strictly to improve the product's appeal to owners. For dogs, smell is the primary means of evaluating palatability. Artificial ingredients may not harm your Poodle, but no one needs more chemicals in his diet.

Minimum and maximum standards for various ingredients are designated as crude protein, crude fat on pet food labels. These levels are established by a panel of animal nutritionists known as the Association of American Feed Control Officials (AAFCO). An AAFCO guaranteed analysis should appear on every commercially manufactured dog food. AAFCO permits ingredients

Helpful Hints

Tips for Choosing Dog Foods

General nutritional guidelines will help you choose a healthy diet for your Poodle, but every dog is an individual. His diet and portion size must be tailored to his needs. The following questions will help you select a suitable food for your dog:

Does he enthusiastically consume his food?

Is his weight within normal limits?

Does he have good muscle tone, healthy skin, and a nice coat?

Is he energetic?

Is the food affordable and convenient to prepare and serve?

to be evaluated in two ways, which will be stated on the label. Controlled feeding trials are the preferred method. In this case, the food has been fed to at least six dogs for at least six months to confirm that the formula provides complete and balanced nutrition. Chemical analysis of the formula is also acceptable, but this method will only establish the levels of specific nutrients in the food. It will not reveal whether the formula is balanced, or if the ingredients are nutritionally accessible to dogs.

AAFCO certifies only two kinds of dog food formulas, growth formulas for puppies and maintenance formulas for adults. Other designations found on labeling—such as senior formulas, weight control formulas, joint care formulas—and premium formulas are not officially recognized.

Supplements

Seek your veterinarian's advice before adding supplements to your Poodle's diet. Excessive doses of most vitamins are simply excreted by the body. Others are retained and can build up to toxic levels or block the absorption of other necessary nutrients.

This can result in a simultaneous shortage of several nutrients. In the short term, the resulting symptoms are frequently nonspecific, but the dog's health and performance will be compromised.

Natural and Organic Foods

Organic pet foods often cost three times as much as conventional formulas, but this alone does not guarantee that they are superior. Any food can be advertised as natural, green, or organic, but only those free of preservatives, pesticides, hormones, and antibiotics may carry the USDA Organic seal. To be labeled as 100 percent organic, a food must contain only organically produced ingredients. Current AAFCO regulations make this impossible for dry dog foods, because the vitamins and minerals added to these formulas during manufacture cannot be organically produced. Foods labeled "Organic" must contain 95 percent organic ingredients. Foods labeled "Made with Organic Ingredients" must contain at least 70 percent organic ingredients.

This is not the only factor to consider. Some organic formulas contain lower percentages of meat protein simply because organically raised meat is extremely expensive. If most of the protein in the food is derived from organic grains and vegetables, this may not be the best diet for your Poodle.

Vegetarian Pet Foods

In reasonable quantities, vegetables and grains provide important nutrients in your Poodle's diet. However, moderation is the key. Dogs are not prone to the same diet-related health issues as humans. Therefore, a vegetarian diet offers no benefits in terms of reducing cholesterol levels or forestalling cardiovascular disease. Because they have a much shorter digestive tract, dogs cannot extract nutrients from raw or undercooked grains and vegetables. The biggest drawback to a canine vegan or vegetarian diet is the fact that dogs must consume an enormous and varied amount of food to ensure adequate nutrition. This will inevitably include much more fiber than necessary. Especially for small dogs, high levels of fiber can lead to nutritional deficiencies, as reduced gastrointestinal transit time limits the absorption of nutrients.

Raw Food Diets

The BARF diet, alternately known as the Biologically Appropriate Raw Food or Bones and Raw Food diet, was formulated by Australian veterinarian Ian Billinghurst. In the belief that cooking and processing destroyed important nutrients, he attempted to re-create a diet of the natural foods that dogs had thrived on for thousands of years.

CAUTION

Raw meat, vegetables, and eggs are potential sources of bacterial contamination. Wash produce carefully and follow food safety procedures when handling and serving raw meat.

Advocates claim that raw foods reduce periodontal disease, skin problems, diabetes, orthopedic problems, cancer, and digestive upsets. To date, no long-term studies have been conducted to confirm or refute the benefits.

Even though raw food diets have become quite popular, there is continuing controversy about the value and safety of feeding raw bones. Most commonly, raw meaty bones are offered whole. This can create risks of choking, intestinal blockage, and tooth damage. Some adherents feed raw turkey or chicken necks. Others grind the bones before feeding. Newer variations of the BARF diet supplement the raw meat and bones with combinations of vegetables, cheese, eggs, yogurt, kibble, and supplements. Commercially formulated frozen raw food diets are also available.

If you choose to feed your Poodle a raw diet, consult your veterinarian and do your research to ensure that it contains the proper ratios of nutrients. The effects of deficiencies, imbalances, or over-supplementation accumulate slowly and may not become obvious for many months.

Poodle Health Issues

Your first line of defense against Poodle health issues is to acquire your dog from a breeder who routinely health tests for genetically based disorders. Many of these cannot be detected in puppies. They do not surface until a dog is middle aged or older, and can only be eliminated by carefully screening each generation of breeding stock. Annual health checks are your next line of defense. They ensure that minor problems are spotted and treated before they compromise your dog's health. Finally, your alertness as a responsible owner is key to protecting your Poodle's health. Any unusual changes in his normal demeanor, energy level, appetite, or personality should merit a trip to veterinarian.

Recommended Health Screening

Hip dysplasia, progressive retinal atrophy, cataracts, thyroid disorders, Cushing's disease, and von Willebrand's disease have been documented in all three Poodle varieties. Toy and Miniature Poodles can also develop Legg-Perthes disease and luxating patellae. Standard Poodles may be afflicted with gastric torsion (bloat), sebaceous adenitis, and Addison's disease.

Addison's Disease Addison's disease is the common name for hypoadrenocorticism, or adrenal insufficiency. Three forms of this autoimmune disease can affect middle-aged dogs: primary, secondary, and atypical. Primary and atypical Addison's are usually caused by immune-mediated damage to the adrenal glands. The primary form can be a complication of a tumor or disease. Secondary hypoadrenocorticism results when the pituitary gland fails to stimulate the adrenal glands with adrenocorticotropic hormone (ACTH).

Early stages are characterized by intermittent lethargy and weakness, vomiting, diarrhea, diminished appetite, and abdominal pain. As the disease progresses these episodes become more severe and frequent. Continued deterioration of the adrenal glands eventually leads to an acute episode known as an Addisonian crisis. Elevated potassium levels will cause irregular heartbeat and a sudden drop in blood pressure.

Addison's disease is diagnosed through blood tests to determine sodium/potassium ratios and blood cortisol levels. The disease can be medically managed with replacement doses of aldosterone—the hormone responsible for maintaining electrolyte levels and cortisol, or glucocorticoids, which are normally secreted by the adrenals.

Cushing's Disease Hyperadrenocorticism, commonly known as Cushing's disease, is a condition that results in overproduction of the hormone cortisol, a natural steroid produced and stored by the adrenal glands. It helps the body function under stress, regulate weight, and maintain tissue. Excessive cortisol compromises immune function, leaving the body vulnerable to diseases and infections.

Cushing's disease typically occurs in middle-aged to older dogs. It is characterized by excessive eating, drinking, urination, lethargy, abdominal enlargement, and thinning coat. The most common form of the disease, pituitary-dependent Cushing's, accounts for 80–85 percent of all cases. It is caused by a slow-growing tumor in the pituitary gland, which triggers overproduction of ACTH. This, in turn, stimulates the adrenal glands to produce more cortisol than necessary.

Non-pituitary Cushing's, accounting for 15–20 percent of cases, is caused by a tumor in one or both adrenal glands, which again leads to excessive production of cortisol. The least common form results from long-term use of cortisone drugs.

Blood tests to diagnose the disease will differentiate between the pituitary and adrenal forms. Ultrasound can be used to detect adrenal tumors. Although Cushing's is typically a lifelong condition, it can be managed with medications, which vary depending on the form of the disease. In December 2008, the Food and Drug Administration (FDA) approved the first drug in more than ten years to treat Cushing's disease in dogs, Vetoryl (trilostane). It blocks the production of cortisol in the adrenal glands and is approved to treat both pituitary- and adrenal-dependent forms of the disease.

Anipryl (selegiline) is also FDA-approved to treat pituitary-dependent Cushing's. A human chemotherapy drug, Lysodren (mitotane), is also used off-label to treat Cushing's in dogs. However, dogs can respond unpredict-ably and experience side effects when taking this drug, so it requires careful monitoring.

Hypothyroidism Hypothyroidism is the most common endocrine disorder in dogs. Insufficient production of thyroid hormone adversely affects many biochemical functions, eventually impacting every body sys-tem. Because the disease progresses slowly, early signs may go unnoticed. Common symptoms include weight gain; dull, thinning coat; darkening skin pigment; symmetrical hair loss on the body; recurring ear infections; and behavioral changes such as lethargy and irritability.

Diagnosis is based on a combination of physical symptoms and blood test-ing, but fluctuating hormone levels can complicate the diagnosis. Lacking conclusive test results, many veterinarians prescribe thyroid replacement therapy for six to eight weeks. If hypothyroidism is the problem, the symp-toms will subside noticeably during this time.

Hip Dysplasia Canine hip dysplasia, a hereditary disease that causes deterioration of the ball-and-socket joint of the hip, has been documented since 1935. It leads to pain and lameness, which can range from impercep-tible to debilitating. The severity of the condition is determined by X-ray evaluation of the hip joints. Poodles should be evaluated for hip dysplasia before breeding, but they must be at least 18 months of age before their test results can be entered in a database. Hip X-rays can be evaluated by the fol-lowing registries:

- Orthopedic Foundation for Animals (OFA)
- PennHIP Program
- Institute for Genetic Disease Control in Animals (GDC)

Researchers are currently developing DNA tests that will allow for fast, accurate diagnosis of hip dysplasia in puppies.

Legg-Calvé-Perthes Disease Legg-Calvé-Perthes disease, a degenera-tion of the hip joint, is most common in dogs weighing less than 25 pounds. Symptoms usually appear between 4 and 12 months of age, with 7 months being the most common age of onset. Bone degeneration leads to muscle atrophy and pronounced pain and limping. It usually occurs in one hip, but 10 to 15 percent of LCP-affected dogs show signs of the disease in both hips.

Diagnosis is confirmed by X-ray, although researchers are developing a DNA test that will make it possible to detect carriers. About one quarter of affected dogs recover with four to six months of restricted activity, which allows the joint to heal. Surgical repair is recommended for severe cases. Surgery involves removing the damaged joint and allowing the hip to form a false joint. Full recovery can take several months to a year.

Patellar Luxation Patellar luxation, or instability of the kneecap, is the most common orthopedic disorder in Poodles. It can be caused by injury, but most cases are the result of malformations of the joint, weak ligaments, misaligned tendons and muscles, or shallow grooves holding the tendons in place. The result is intermittent or permanent dislocation of the kneecap.

FYI: What Is a CERF Exam?

A CERF (Canine Eye Registry Foundation) exam is performed by a veterinary ophthalmologist to detect common eye disorders. The exam includes an assessment of eye shape and size, mobility of the eyeball, positioning of eyelids, lens clarity, blink response, corneal reflex, symmetry of pupil size, and the presence of any opacities, lesions, or inflammation. For some breeds, additional tests to measure tear production or eye pressure are also performed. The results of annual CERF testing are maintained in the CERF registry.

Most often, one leg is affected, but 25 percent of cases show signs of the problem in both legs, although severity can vary.

Occasional partial dislocation will cause the dog to hop for a few steps until the kneecap pops back into place. Permanent dislocation immobilizes the joint, and the dog loses the use of that leg. Patellar luxation can be diagnosed during a routine veterinary exam. X-rays are not necessary except to determine the extent of the defect in severe cases. Some cases will benefit from surgery to stabilize the joint, but luxations caused by injury or complicated by secondary joint disease may not respond well to surgical correction.

Toys and Miniatures should be OFA-certified as free of this problem before breeding.

Progressive Retinal Atrophy Progressive retinal atrophy (PRA) denotes several diseases that lead to gradual deterioration of the retina and, eventually, blindness. Seven types of PRA have been documented in dogs. Unfortunately, there is no treatment or cure.

The most common form documented in Miniature and Toy Poodles is progressive rod-cone degeneration (prcd). It is usually diagnosed around three years of age. Some affected dogs retain some useful vision throughout their life, while others progress to blindness in mid-life.

All Poodles should be certified free of PRA before breeding. This examination must be done annually, and testing results must be registered with the Canine Eye Registry Foundation (CERF). DNA testing is available to identify Toys and Miniatures that are affected or carrying the gene for prcd-PRA. Results of DNA testing can be recorded in the OFA database.

Cataracts Any opacity of the lens is technically a cataract, whether it is confined to a tiny area or entirely covers the lens. Cortical cataracts develop in the cortex or outside layers of the lens. These generally progress from the outside edges to the center of the lens, necessitating lens removal. Capsular cataracts, which form in the covering of the lens, and nuclear cataracts, which form in the center, are non-progressive.

Cataracts should not be confused with the age-related bluish or whitish tinge to the eye, known as nuclear sclerosis. With this condition, the iris and cornea remain clearly visible.

Cataracts in dogs under age eight are classified as congenital or juvenile. Congenital cataracts are present at birth but don't become noticeable until several weeks later, when the iris turns from blue to its adult color. Juvenile cataracts, which develop between birth and age six, are usually progressive. Some cases of congenital and juvenile cataracts disappear on their own, by one year of age. This is known as resorption, but it is unpredictable and, rather than improved vision, may lead to ocular inflammation or glaucoma. Late-onset cataracts develop after age six, and their frequency rises with age.

Sebaceous Adenitis (SA) Sebaceous adenitis (SA) is a skin disease characterized by inflammation of the sebaceous glands. Common symptoms are dandruff, known as scaling, progressive hair loss, musty skin odor, and secondary skin infections. First identified in veterinary research in 1987, it has been documented in all Standard Poodle colors. A simple autosomal recessive trait, it most commonly strikes young adults. Standard Poodles should be tested for this disorder annually with a skin punch biopsy. Cases may be misdiagnosed as hypothyroidism or allergies, as SA symptoms tend to vary in severity. Currently, there is no cure. Treatment includes frequent bathing with hypoallergenic shampoo to remove scaling and dead hair, along with antibiotic therapy to control secondary skin infections.

CAUTION

Early Signs of GDV

- Gagging, drooling, and repeated unproductive attempts to vomit
- Agitation and restlessness due to obvious discomfort
- Hunched posture, distended abdomen
- Shallow breathing and elevated heart rate
- Pale mucous membranes

Gastric Dilatation-Volvulus (Bloat) Standard Poodles are susceptible to bloat, also known as gastric dilatation-volvulus, or GDV. Dogs between six and nine years of age are at higher risk, especially if closely related family members have had this condition. There are two distinct forms of GDV. *Gastric dilatation* occurs when the stomach becomes distended with a combination of food, water, and gas. It also may twist between the esophagus and the duodenum, trapping the contents and obstructing abdominal blood flow. This leads to a rapid drop in blood pressure, shock, and damage to internal organs. *Bloat* is a life-threatening emergency, which can kill in less than an hour.

If you suspect that your Poodle is suffering from GDV, get him to the veterinarian immediately. Most dogs survive if they receive emergency surgery. Repeated bouts of distension or a family history of GDV could make your dog a candidate for preventative surgery to anchor the stomach in place. You can also take other preventative measures:

- Do not feed your Poodle from elevated dishes. Studies have shown that, rather than preventing bloat, this will increase the risk.
- Prevent your Poodle from gulping large amounts of food. Feed two or three small meals daily, and encourage him to eat slowly.

- Do not allow him to exercise or drink water for one hour after eating.
- Avoid foods containing high levels of fat and carbohydrates, which are more likely to cause intestinal gas.

Von Willebrand's Disease Von Willebrand's disease (vWD) is an inherited bleeding disorder characterized by delayed clotting, comparable to hemophilia in humans. Clotting is the end result of a complex chain of chemical reactions. Dogs suffering from von Willebrand's disease are missing one or more of the substances that cause platelets to form clots. There is no cure, and transfusions are the most common treatment.

Despite controversy regarding its effectiveness, the drug desmopressin acetate (DDAVP) can be administered intranasally, studies suggest, to promote clotting during a bleeding episode. A DNA test is available to identify Poodles affected with, or carrying, the vWD gene.

Spay/Neuter

Unless your Poodle has the potential to improve the breed, he should be neutered. If he was purchased as a pet, neutering was probably required in his sales contract, but it may not stipulate an age for the procedure.

For decades, it has been standard practice to neuter dogs at four or five months of age. In the 1980s, early spay/neuter of pets at eight weeks of age began to gain popularity. This practice also spawned long overdue studies to track the overall health of neutered pets. The findings were surprising. A 2007 study revealed that early neutering can have a long-range negative impact on many aspects of canine health. For more information, see the study, "The Long-Term Health Effects of Spay/Neuter in Dogs" by Laura J. Sanborn, at *www.naiaonline.org/pdfs/LongTermHealthEffectsOfSpayNeuterInDogs.pdf.*

Sex hormones play a significant role in physical and mental maturity as well as reproductive ability. They control bone development and density. Later neutering ensures sturdy bones that are less prone to injury. It also appears to significantly lower the risk of bone cancer. A study by the AKC Canine Health Foundation also showed that, rather than minimizing behavior issues, early neutering seems to exacerbate aggression and fearfulness. Newer recommendations suggest that 12–14 months is the optimum age for this surgery. Although neutering has long been advocated to cure behavior problems, if you have allowed your Poodle to develop bad habits, neutering will not provide a quick fix.

Parasites

Don't assume that your Poodle has fleas simply because you have seen him scratching. A host of reasons can explain persistent itching. A close inspection will reveal adult fleas or flea grit on his skin if this is actually the problem. You can confirm that fleas have invaded your home by placing a bowl of soapy water under a night-light in a darkened room. This will not control fleas, but it is an effective way to monitor the situation. If you find one flea, rest assured there are more. Interrupting the flea life cycle requires ridding the dog and his environment of adult fleas, immature fleas, and flea eggs.

Adults spend their entire lives on their host, and a topical flea treatment is the fastest, easiest way to take care of them. These treatments, the latest innovation in the war on fleas, were formerly available only by prescription. Although they are now available over the counter, they should be used under your veterinarian's supervision. Regardless of where they are purchased, flea control products are toxic chemicals. Fleas on your Poodle will die over several hours after you apply the treatment. However, newly hatched fleas will continue to replace them for two weeks as they emerge from cocoons in the environment. They will be killed when they jump on the dog.

You must also take steps to rid the environment of flea eggs. Twice a week, thoroughly wash dog bedding in hot, soapy water and run it through a hot dryer to kill immature fleas. Hot steam cleaning will kill immature fleas in upholstery and carpets. After cleaning, apply an insect growth regulator to carpeted areas to prevent a fresh wave of fleas from reproducing. Even if you have won the battle at home, your Poodle can pick up new fleas if he comes in contact with infested wildlife, such as stray cats or raccoons.

Ticks

If your Poodle spends any time in grass or wooded areas, he is a potential candidate for ticks. They are easy to miss when they first climb aboard your pet, but once they become embedded they can grow to ten times their original size, making them quite easy to spot.

Most ticks are detected during routine grooming, and early removal is important. Some ticks carry diseases, most notably Lyme disease. However, they must feed for several hours before transferring pathogens to their host. If you find a tick on your Poodle, grasp it with tweezers, a hemostat, or a tick key and pull it straight out, being careful that the mouthparts are not left in the dog's skin. If not removed, they can lead to an infection at the site of the tick bite.

You can apply a skin disinfectant after removal, but never apply kerosene, gasoline, or lit matches to your dog's skin to remove a tick or disinfect the area. Store the tick in the freezer or a container of alcohol in case you need to have it tested later on. Symptoms of tick-transmitted diseases include fever, lethargy, and enlarged lymph nodes, and may appear weeks after a dog is bitten. If you suspect your Poodle has contracted a tick-borne disease, a blood test can confirm this.

Mange

The most common type of mange is produced by *Demodex canis*, a microscopic mite found in the hair follicles of most dogs. Mange occurs most frequently in young puppies and senior dogs, whose immature or weakened immune systems allow mites to proliferate. The classic symptoms are itchy, red scaly patches on the face, feet, and legs, but mange can spread to other parts of the body. Diagnosis is confirmed by a quick, inexpensive skin scraping done at your veterinarian's office. Treatment is less straightforward. It must be continued for at least three months, and often long after symptoms have disappeared, to eradicate all of the mites.

Heartworm Preventative

Heartworm was once confined to tropical climates but has now been documented in dogs throughout the country. Year-round preventative may not be necessary unless you live in a warm climate where mosquitoes are prevalent all year round. Daily or weekly heartworm medications have been replaced by more convenient monthly preventatives. These formulations also combat other internal parasites, such as roundworms, hookworms, and whipworms. Your dog should always be blood tested to ensure he is not harboring heartworms before beginning preventative medication.

First Aid

Every dog owner should keep a first aid kit stocked and ready in case of emergencies, which can range from a digestive upset to a dog bite. Many minor health issues can be treated at home. However, it can be difficult to judge the severity of various health disorders without some knowledge of first aid. A pet first aid manual or course is a worthwhile investment. It may save your Poodle's life, and it will certainly lessen your anxiety about confronting a medical emergency. You are more capable of recognizing a life-threatening emergency if you know how to assess your dog's vital signs.

Knowing how to treat shock, staunch bleeding, or administer CPR can make a crucial difference in the minutes before you reach your veterinarian. Consult your veterinarian for dosage recommendations for over-the-counter medications. Contact information for your veterinarian and the nearest veterinary emergency clinic should be in your cell phone, near your home phone, and in your first aid kit.

10 **Questions** Does Your Poodle Have a Healthy Lifestyle

Have you trained and socialized your Poodle? Believe it or not, behavior problems stemming from incomplete training and socialization are the leading cause of death in young adult dogs. Untrained dogs are more likely to suffer traumatic accidents. More frequently, they are surrendered to animal shelters because the owners are unable to cope with their chronic misbehavior.

Is your Poodle microchipped? A microchip is a tiny silicon radio transponder implanted under the skin. Lost and stolen pets have been returned months or years later thanks to this form of identification. Each chip contains a unique identification number, which is read by a small handheld scanner.

Your Poodle's chip number must be entered into a national database, preferably one that cross-references information with other microchip companies. If you report your dog missing, employees at the microchip company should flag his number in case they are contacted by someone trying to trace it. Some companies require annual renewal fees to maintain your pet's information in their databases, or charge an additional fee to amend your contact information.

Is your Poodle adequately protected against contagious diseases? Most veterinarians now recommend that dogs receive booster shots every three years rather than annually. Some vaccines trigger long-lasting immunity, while others do not. Your veterinarian can assess your Poodle's immune status through an antibody titer test in order to decide when revaccination is needed. Excessive or unnecessary vaccinations will not

boost your dog's immune response. In fact, they may have quite the opposite effect.

A tailored vaccination schedule is the best way to provide optimum protection and minimal risk. The value of non-core, optional vaccines depends on your dog's level of risk. If specific diseases are prevalent in your area, such as Lyme disease, leptospirosis, and giardia, it may be advisable to vaccinate against them. Do your own research and discuss this with your Poodle's breeder and your veterinarian.

Are you ready and willing to visit your Poodle's veterinarian? A veterinarian's skill and experience will be of no use to your Poodle if you are uncomfortable asking questions or volunteering information. Your Poodle may not require yearly vaccinations, but an annual checkup is the best way to spot impending health issues. Early detection and intervention can make a major difference in your dog's ability to fully recover from an illness. For instance, symptoms of hypothyroidism can be variable and subtle, but the disease can have a major impact on your Poodle's quality of life. Likewise, without routine testing, internal parasites may go unnoticed.

Is your Poodle free from internal and external parasites? Fleas and flea dirt are easy to spot during routine grooming and examinations. Along with severe itching, flea bites can cause severe allergic reactions known as flea bite dermatitis. This allergic response to flea saliva leads to intense itching and swelling. It usually causes the dog to dig and scratch at the flea bite, leading to skin abrasions, hot spots, coat loss, and possible infections. Treatment includes combinations of medications: topical and oral antibiotics, medicated shampoos, steroids, and antihistamines.

Fleas also serve as an intermediate host for tapeworms. If your dog has fleas, there is a very good chance that his health is also being compromised by internal parasites.

 Are your Poodle's teeth cleaned regularly? Periodontal disease is another silent threat to your dog's health. Most dogs experience little discomfort until this problem has advanced to severe infection and tooth loss.

Dental chews or hard kibble are not sufficient to scrape plaque and tartar from teeth. Train your Poodle to accept having his teeth brushed. Start by rubbing your finger over his teeth and gums. When he is accustomed to this, add a bit of doggy toothpaste to your fingertip. When he willingly tolerates this step, gently brush his teeth with a doggy toothbrush or gauze pad. You can also apply plaque-preventing gel to your dog's teeth each week. Heavy tartar accumulation and any resulting complications, like gum infection or fractured teeth, must be treated by a veterinarian.

 Do you minimize your Poodle's exposure to environmental toxins? Low levels of dangerous chemicals lurk everywhere in our environment. Because our pets spend so much time in our homes, their exposure to household chemicals is much more intense. Dogs also have more opportunities to ingest contaminants by licking, chewing, self-grooming, inhalation, or skin absorption.

Make yourself aware of hidden chemical additives by reading the labels on food, treats, bedding, and grooming products.

 Does your Poodle's lifestyle minimize stress? Numerous human studies confirm that stress compromises immune function, thereby increasing susceptibility to a host of diseases. Poor diet and parasite infestation are obvious factors that will physically stress a dog's constitution. Anxiety and boredom can have the same effect.

If your Poodle is poorly equipped to cope with social encounters, this will become a lifelong source of cumulative stress. Likewise, a lack of mental challenges will leave him bored and anxious.

 Does your Poodle exercise regularly? Exercise can forestall and minimize many mental and physical age-related problems. Regular exercise maintains muscle mass and bone density, and loosens up tight ligaments and stiff joints. Daily exercise also plays a role in your Poodle's ongoing mental health by giving him something to look forward to. It lifts his spirits and improves blood flow to his brain.

 Is your Poodle overweight? Obesity raises the odds that your Poodle will develop arthritis, spinal disc disease, cardiovascular disease, urinary disorders, or cancer. His nutritional needs and metabolism change throughout his life. Puppies require almost twice as many calories as adults, and senior dogs require 20 percent fewer total calories than middle-aged dogs to maintain their ideal weight. Make sure to monitor your Poodle's weight and regularly adjust his calorie intake.

Chapter Seven

Training and Activities

It's nearly impossible to separate this breed from the image of immaculately coiffed show dogs and pampered pets. In reality, Poodles are first and foremost versatile working dogs, with the keen instincts, drive, intelligence, and athleticism of their water dog ancestors. Don't be deceived by appearances: Poodles have the potential to excel in activities that you might not associate with this breed.

Training and Socialization

You probably envision your Poodle sharing your life as a beloved member of your family. Although puppies and new dogs require close supervision, you are also probably assuming that this is a temporary measure. But easing up on supervision won't be possible unless you have equipped your Poodle with the skills to behave in a socially acceptable manner. If you want to give your Poodle freedom, socialization and training are mandatory. He must become adaptable and accept variations in his routine. He must develop social skills to interact politely and communicate properly with humans and other dogs. He must cultivate self-control in order to channel his energy appropriately and curb impulsive behavior. He must accept spending time alone without suffering undue anxiety.

Without frequent positive social encounters, he is likely to react defensively toward anyone unfamiliar. Regularly introduce him to strangers who are willing to call him by name, give him treats, and create a positive impression. As he develops friendships and uses his social skills in new situations, his confidence will grow. He will behave appropriately because his actions will not be motivated by confusion or anxiety.

Some owners prize perfectly trained pets. Others prefer playful, unexpected behavior from their dogs. Most want something in between, a well-behaved Poodle with the spontaneity to be a fun companion. However, very few owners enjoy living with a dog that routinely destroys the house, enrages the neighbors, or spends half his time at the veterinarian recovering from injuries incurred through reckless behavior. Up to a point, you will probably ignore or tolerate things like excessive barking, destructive chewing, or imperfect housetraining. Your Poodle will learn to disregard your confusing signals, and discipline will disintegrate. The day will come when someone in your household loses patience and overreacts when he disobeys once too often. The dog will bear the brunt of recrimination, not the irresponsible person who allowed these habits to flourish.

Saying No

Every Poodle must learn the concept of *no,* but this must be done with forethought and purpose. Poodles devote substantial mental energy to examining events and drawing conclusions. Perhaps you have watched your dog cock his leg on the rubber tree plant and ignored this indiscretion for weeks.

Fun Facts

Poodle Versatility

Alaska native John Suter bought three Standard Poodles in 1976. During the next two decades, he bred six generations of Poodles with the goal of utilizing them as sled dogs. His Poodles competed in 280 races, and finished first, second, or third place 90 times. In 1988, Suter placed 38th out of 52 starters in the Iditarod with a part-Poodle team. He finished this grueling 1,100-mile race with all-Poodle teams in 1989, 1990, and 1991.

Maybe you were busy or distracted. Maybe you were reluctant to undermine your bond by scolding him. Regardless of the reason, he is justified in thinking that it is okay to water the plants. An explosive overreaction after tolerating this behavior for weeks will not instantly revise his learned behavior pattern. Instead, it can worsen behavior issues by making him fearful, anxious, and defensive.

Corrections must be appropriate to the deed. Poodles are sensitive and quick to react to human emotions. They are hardwired to respond to subtle social signals in order to avoid aggressive confrontations. In most situations, a stern word or glance gets the message across.

Corrections must also be done consistently. Poodles have long memories. If your dog does not understand why he is being reprimanded, he is likely to become resentful and withdrawn. The easiest way to avoid confusion is by never allowing him to ignore you. If you ask him to stop barking or jumping and he doesn't respond, take the time to follow through, rather than simply letting his misbehavior slide. Consistent messages have another benefit. They reassure him of his place in your pack. His resulting sense of security bolsters his confidence and strengthens his trust in you.

Good timing is integral to effective corrections. Your response must coincide with the misbehavior. Otherwise, your Poodle can easily make a different association about your unhappy reaction. If more than a few seconds elapse, there is no guarantee that his interpretation of the events will be linked to the crime. Condition yourself to anticipate your Poodle's intentions to water the rubber tree plant. This way you can respond with a well-timed *no* before it happens.

Training Classes

Training classes not only provide an introduction to basic commands, they can be great opportunities for socialization and an educational resource for owners. They can also create a huge setback in your Poodle's training. The atmosphere of the class and the methodology of the instructor will have a big impact on his learning curve and his personality. Obviously, you want a class that features positive, gentle methods. At the same time, the instructor must be able to maintain control. The class size should be limited to approximately 12 dog/handler teams per instructor to ensure that everyone receives individual attention. Each team should have enough space to avoid feeling crowded or distracted by other participants. Typically, the instructor introduces a new lesson each week, provides a demonstration, and practices new techniques with each team individually. This may be followed by a discussion period, where owners can seek advice and compare notes.

National organizations offer various dog trainer certifications, but there are no recognized requirements in this field. Paper credentials may not

105

FYI: Clicker Training

Clicker training has been around since the 1940s, when trainers began using it as a behavior reinforcement tool. It did not achieve widespread acceptance until the 1990s, when the noted trainer Karen Pryor popularized the technique through her seminars and books.

Basically, a specific behavior is singled out by a clicking sound produced by a small noisemaker, and immediately rewarded by praise and treats. Although the click essentially serves the same purpose as *good boy,* the click has an immediate subconscious effect on the dog's learning curve. Partly, this is because the click sound is unique, which sends a precise message to the dog. It also prevents the dog from becoming distracted or confused by ambiguous hand signals, vocal prompts, or improperly timed rewards. Most important, the clicker improves a trainer's timing by providing an immediate response to desired behavior.

You will need a clicker and a generous supply of very tiny, tasty treats, like chopped bits of cheese, hot dog, or chicken. Avoid foods that require a lot of chewing.

Begin training in an area that is relatively free from distractions. Start by clicking and immediately rewarding your dog with a treat the second he pays attention to the click. Click only once, and do not follow up with praise or prompts. Most dogs make this connection after 10–15 repetitions.

At that point, he will anticipate a treat every time he hears the clicker. This response can be used to shape virtually any behavior, such as training your Poodle to sit up on command.

Get your dog's attention and follow up with a few click/treat rewards to get him on your page. At this point, he will be waiting for the next click/treat and you can start getting choosy about the behavior you reward. Your Poodle will probably run through a whole repertoire of actions trying to elicit a click/treat. He might bark, jump, nuzzle, or spin around. Ignore all of these. Eventually he will do something associated with sitting up, such as sitting or raising his paw. Bingo! Click and treat. Now you will almost see the wheels turning as he tries to figure out exactly how he earned the click. He will experiment and eventually display another behavior associated with sitting up. Click and treat again.

Don't be tempted to help him or repeatedly click. Give one click and one treat for the right behavior; otherwise he will get confused. Poodles have excellent problem-solving skills and generally respond enthusiastically to this training method.

translate into competent skills. Your choice of a trainer should be based on an individual's experience and ability, rather than a reputation built on giving advice. Most important, the trainer should demonstrate a rapport with your dog. If your Poodle fails to respond positively to a trainer or seems diffident, this may not be a good match.

Basic Training

Unless new information is linked to immediate survival, most dogs require several weeks to process complex ideas and move them from short-term to long-term memory. Poodles often manage this much faster. Set high standards for your Poodle, but maintain realistic expectations. If he is slow to grasp a new concept, do not lower your expectations. Break the lesson down into smaller parts and give him plenty of opportunities to practice each new behavior in different situations. Don't move to the next step until he has mastered the previous one. If he begins to lose focus, backtrack. Vary new lessons with a refresher course on the basics. This not only reinforces familiar concepts, it provides a tremendous confidence boost for him.

Keep lessons short and upbeat. Your Poodle won't enjoy them if you don't. Your body language, expression, and voice should convey encouragement and friendliness. If you are cranky and impatient, he will sense this and respond accordingly. When first teaching a new concept, work in a small area free of distractions. It will defeat the purpose of training if he has the option of running off and ignoring you. As his attention and understanding improve, so will his ability to focus and ignore distractions.

Helpful Hints

A clicker can be an excellent tool to quiet an overexcited barker. The click will refocus his attention away from whatever prompted his barking. It's also impossible for him to eat treats and bark at the same time. Tell him to sit or lie down and be quiet, and give a treat. Repeat this until he calms down.

Your Poodle may seem well trained at a young age, but training is not a job to be completed and checked off the list. Regular training is an integral part of your relationship. To your Poodle, this is his work in life, and everyone needs to know that his work has purpose. Vary serious training with fun activities. For some Poodles this might be retrieving work. Others love clicker training. Very few Poodles can resist the admiration of an audience enthralled by their repertoire of tricks.

Behavior Problems

From your Poodle's perspective, many of the activities you label as bad habits are simply normal expressions of canine behavior. You can modify instinctive behaviors like chewing, barking, jumping, and begging through training, but you must accept the fact that they are bundled with the software of every canine brain.

Chewing

Chewing is the canine equivalent of doing crosswords or knitting. It is a relaxing pastime, designed to relieve boredom and lift the spirits. Every dog enjoys chewing, but some breeds cultivate this habit more obsessively, and most retrievers fall into this group. The good news is that Poodles are very good at differentiating between objects. Your Poodle can learn to chew his toys instead of your new leather handbag. However, this will not happen without your intervention. Keep temptations out of his reach, supervise carefully, and interrupt him before he can get started on the chair leg. Tell him "*No*," redirect him to a chew toy, and always praise him for chewing on something appropriate. Doing this consistently will teach him to forego forbidden items. For some dogs, deterrents like bitter apple will discourage inappropriate chewing. They are not always effective, however, because chewing is also an outlet to relieve stress or boredom. Your Poodle may be telling you that he needs some changes in his routine.

Barking

Poodles possess a fairly strong protective instinct, and even Toys will sound the alarm when they notice something amiss in their territory. This could range from the daily mail delivery to a prowler climbing in the window. Obviously, some situations warrant more barking than others. He's doing his job to warn you, and it's your responsibility to take over from there. Check it out, calmly reassure him that all is well, and let him know that no further barking is needed. Barking can easily get out of hand if you do not respond consistently and correctly.

Chronic barking can be caused by anxiety, boredom, or loneliness. Efforts to quiet him down won't be effective unless you identify the underlying cause and revise the primary behavior issue. He may need more socialization, exercise, personal attention, or a more structured daily routine. Don't inadvertently encourage excessive barking by responding to your Poodle's demands for attention. If he barks when overexcited, a loud emotional reaction from you will encourage him further.

Excessive barking is a major source of dog complaints, so it's equally important to modify his environment to discourage the habit. This might include keeping the curtains closed, planting shrubs to block his view of outdoor distractions, moving his crate or bed to a quiet area of your home, or never leaving him outdoors alone.

Jumping Up

Poodles are equally comfortable on two legs or four. Their excellent sense of balance and love of human attention can easily combine to create a chronic jumping problem. Puppies instinctively jump for attention. If this is ignored or rewarded, the behavior becomes habitual—no amount of yelling or leash-jerking will stop it. Overreacting is likely to worsen the situation and get him even more excited. Traditional deterrents, like kneeing the dog in the chest or stepping on his toes, are easily misinterpreted by Poodles. If he becomes frightened or anxious, he will seek reassurance, which can also lead to more jumping.

If he usually launches himself at you when you arrive home, act calm and reserved, and avoid cues that could trigger a jumping frenzy. Greet him only when he approaches you politely with all four feet on the floor. Equally annoying is the Poodle who wildly jumps on guests. If he appears poised to tackle a guest, get your hands on his collar and tell him "*Sit*." Instruct visitors to ignore him until he settles down. At that point, they can ask him to sit for a treat, but interactions should remain subdued.

Everyone in your family must reinforce the importance of polite greetings by reacting in the same way if he jumps for attention. Ignore wild behavior and reward calmness. His jumping may intensify at first, but after a few weeks he will lose interest. This doesn't mean he's forgotten about it, however. It only takes one or two payoffs to reestablish this habit. Consistency is essential.

Begging

Persistent begging can result from ignoring or encouraging problematic behaviors until they get out of hand. Dogs instinctively search for food in their environment; this is a survival mechanism. However, they perfect their methods through trial and error. Poodles are quick learners. If a particular behavior gets results, he will repeat it and refine it endlessly. This includes staring, pawing, and whining to get a taste of your food. It can also extend to jumping on the table or grabbing food off of your plate. These habits are not just annoying; dogs can accidentally ingest dangerous items or choke while bolting down stolen treats.

Before bringing a new dog into your home, decide if he will share your mealtime or eat separately. Varying this rule is the basis of most begging problems. If you want your Poodle in the room during dinner, teach him proper table manners. You will have no problem maintaining his rapt attention while you eat. Use these opportunities to reinforce the idea that tactics like whining, drooling, and demanding food don't work. Instead, ask him to sit or lie quietly beside your chair and praise that behavior instead. If you choose to give him a taste of food, teach him to take it gently. If he lunges for it, move it out of his reach and tell him no. Poodles are too smart to pursue a strategy that never pays off. Of course, this system will only work if your Poodle receives the same response from every member of the household.

Dog Sports and Activities

Poodles learn quickly, enjoy challenges, and have successfully competed in just about every dog sport. On an amateur level, there are plenty of activities you can share with your Poodle. If you envision a serious competitive career, your canine partner must possess the mental and physical resources for these pursuits.

A good candidate for competitive sports is not overly dominant or timid around people and other dogs. He should exhibit a confident, stable

Breed Needs

Grooming for Sports

Poodles can be shown in any trim for sports, and the most popular choices are sporting and retriever trims. However, as author Gervase Markham advised centuries ago, Poodle trims and coat length should be suited to weather conditions and terrain. A short clip minimizes problems like mats and burrs, but a dog may benefit from the protection of a longer coat in rough terrain or cold weather. Regardless of coat length, check your Poodle for burrs, foxtails, injuries, and ticks after every outdoor run. If he's willing to wear one, a nylon jumpsuit can also help to protect his coat.

demeanor, not easily ruffled, and be quick to recover from surprises. He should willingly investigate new things and eagerly accompany you in unfamiliar situations. Dogs who love chasing and retrieving toys generally have the potential to excel in sports. Reluctant dogs can be taught to retrieve, but those with a strong natural drive typically have a higher motivation for training and competition. An affinity for water is another indication of strong retriever instincts; your poodle should be curious rather than fearful around water. Most of all, your Poodle must be unfailingly responsive to you and

totally reliable off lead before commencing a sport. It's not unusual for normally well-behaved dogs to lose focus when caught up in the excitement.

Conditioning for Sports

No matter his determination, your Poodle won't get far without the strength and stamina for these activities. Before commencing any sport or training program, he should have a checkup to ensure that his hips, elbows, knees, heart, and eyes are healthy. He should then be gradually conditioned for strenuous exercise. Most sports require both strength and flexibility, and his conditioning routine should alternate activities to build strength, stamina, flexibility, and coordination. A conditioning period also gives you time to gain needed confidence in a new sport. Poodles can sense when their owner is unsure, and this will interfere with their performance.

A 30-minute exercise session three times a week is a good start for a conditioning program. The session could include 20 minutes of trotting, or 10 minutes of swimming, for an aerobic workout, plus a 10-minute warm-up of stretching exercises and a cool-down period. Gradually lengthen his workout, but never overdo it. An overexerted dog pants heavily and may suddenly run out of steam.

Keep in mind that Poodles mature slowly. Your dog may be eligible to compete at six months of age, but he may not be mentally or physically ready. Puppies should be introduced to basic obedience and sports to build motivation and focus, but don't introduce endurance exercises until six months of age. For puppies, nothing compares to running and play to promote muscle development, bone strength, endurance, and coordination.

After six months, you can introduce a moderate program of jogging, swimming, and free running exercise three times per week. After 18 months of age, you can increase the duration of each activity and safely add jumping exercises.

Agility

The AKC held its first agility trial in 1994, and since then agility has become the club's most popular competitive sport. It's challenging, exciting, and equally entertaining for participants and spectators. It is also mentally and physically demanding for both dog and handler. Agility trials are designed to test a dog's versatility and ability to cooperate with a human partner. It's not surprising that many Poodles become agility stars.

The objective is to negotiate an obstacle course within a time limit. Agility scores reflect speed and accuracy. The AKC offers three types of agility classes—standard, jumpers with Weaves, and FAST—with increasingly challenging levels of difficulty to earn Novice, Open, Excellent, and Master titles. All dogs run the same course, but class divisions provide lower jump heights for smaller dogs. Standard Class includes activities such as the dog walk, A-frame, and seesaw. Jumpers with Weaves is faster paced, with only jumps, tunnels, and weave poles. FAST Class is designed to test accuracy, speed, and the dog's ability to respond from a distance. Dogs that have earned Excellent Standard and Excellent Jumpers titles can continue competing for MACH (Master Agility Championship) titles.

Most dogs can compete in agility, and Poodles usually require no coaxing to give it a try. Many training schools offer introductory classes to familiarize dogs and handlers with the various obstacles and the rules of the sport.

Even if you don't have serious aspirations for your Poodle, agility training can be an excellent confidence builder for timid dogs and a fantastic outlet for energetic dogs. It's also a great way to improve your handling skills and build rapport with your Poodle.

Obedience

Competitive obedience has been Poodle territory since the AKC first offered obedience titles in 1936. Eighteen obedience trials were held that year, and 33 Companion Dog (CD) titles were awarded. These were won by nine different breeds, but Standard Poodles took home more than a third, earning 13 CD titles. Three Standards also earned The AKC's first Companion Dog Excellent (CDX) titles by year's end. The following year, four dogs went on to earn AKC's first Utility Dog (UD) titles. At that time, UD exercises also included tracking, which later became a separate AKC title. Despite that, two Standard Poodles qualified for UD titles. One of these dogs, Carillon Epreuve, owned by Helene Whitehouse Walker, also made history as the first dog to earn all three AKC obedience titles. Poodles have held their lead in obedience ever since.

AKC obedience competition is divided into three progressively more difficult levels: Novice, Open, and Utility. At Novice level, dogs compete for the CD title. Exercises include heeling on and off lead, coming when called, standing for examination, and remaining in a long sit or down. Open competition, to earn a Companion Dog Excellent (CDX) title, includes more challenging exercises, like jumping and retrieving. In utility competition, dogs must respond to hand signals, locate articles by scent, retrieve them, and perform jumps on command.

Rather than competing against one another, each dog is measured against an ideal presentation of each exercise, with points deducted for errors. Competitors must finish with at least 170 out of a possible 200 points, and must earn three qualifying scores to earn each title. Titled utility dogs may continue competing for Utility Dog Excellent (UDX) and Obedience Trial Champion (OTCH) titles. Specialty shows also offer non-regular obedience classes such as Brace, Team, and Veteran.

A Miniature, Ch. OTCH MACH Braylane Betty's Bein' Bad UDX TDC VCD3, became the first Poodle to qualify as an AKC Versatile Companion Dog (VCD), earning titles in conformation, obedience, and agility. She went on to earn a tracking title, as well as a VCX in 2006. The first Standard to achieve three VCD titles (VCD3) was Graphic By Popular Demand VCD3 JH MX MXJ.

Tracking

Every dog can detect a scent trail, but a good tracking dog requires natural instinct combined with intelligence, determination, and training. AKC tracking tests are noncompetitive trials designed to evaluate a dog's ability to follow a scent trail and locate specific articles. The tests are not timed, but the dog must actively search or follow a trail throughout the test. Handlers are permitted to offer verbal encouragement, but they may not physically guide or direct their dogs.

Tracking Dog The AKC began offering the Tracking Dog (TD) title in 1947. To qualify, dogs must follow a 440–500-yard scent trail that is 30 minutes to 2 hours old and includes three to five turns.

Tracking Dog Excellent The Tracking Dog Excellent (TDX) title was first offered in 1980. To qualify, dogs must follow a 800–1000-yard scent trail that is 3 to 5 hours old over a variety of ground conditions and obstacles.

Variable Surface Tracking The Variable Surface Tracking (VST) title was introduced in 1995. It is designed to evaluate tracking ability in an urban setting. To qualify, dogs must follow a 600–800-yard course that is 3 to 5 hours old over three different surfaces, including two hard surfaces, such as asphalt, gravel, or concrete.

Rally

Rally was approved as an AKC event in 2005. At that time, it was meant to be a transitional step from basic training to competitive obedience and agility. No one anticipated that it would become a tremendously popular sport in its own right. It's also a great way to introduce your Poodle to the demands of competition.

Scoring is less rigorous than in traditional obedience. Teams are judged on coordination, problem-solving skills, and strategy, rather than on speed or precision. Unlike in obedience, communication between dog and handler is encouraged, and handlers may talk to their dogs and use hand signals. Dog/handler teams navigate the course at their own pace, stopping at stations to perform specific exercises designated on signs at each one. Each team begins with 100 points. Points are deducted for errors, with a minimum score of 70 points needed to qualify. Three qualifying scores are required to earn each title.

As in agility and obedience, the requirements become progressively more challenging at each level.

- Rally Novice (RN) competition consists of 10–15 basic on-lead exercises.
- Rally Advanced (RA) competition consists of 12–17 exercises to demonstrate responsiveness and control off lead.
- Rally Excellent (RE) competition consists of 15–20 off-lead exercises designed to demonstrate precision and coordination between dog and handler.
- RE titled dogs can continue competing for Rally Advanced Excellent (RAE) titles, which are numbered to reflect how many times the dog has qualified at that level.

AKC Hunt Tests

The AKC instituted hunting tests for retrieving breeds in the 1980s, and Standard Poodles became eligible to compete in 1996. Like field trials, retriever hunting tests evaluate natural ability under simulated hunting con-

ACTIVITIES The Canine Good Citizen

The AKC created the Canine Good Citizen (CGC) program in 1989 to encourage responsible dog ownership. Owners must sign the Responsible Dog Owner Pledge, acknowledging their responsibilities regarding their dogs' training and care. The second part of the program consists of exercises performed by dog and owner for a CGC evaluator. They demonstrate the dog's balanced temperament, social skills, and familiarity with basic commands. The CGC exercises include:

- Tolerating attention from a friendly stranger
- Sitting calmly on command
- Willingly cooperating to be groomed
- Heeling on lead
- Walking through a crowd
- Performing *sit* and *stay* on command
- Coming when called
- Responding calmly when approached by another dog
- Tolerating a distraction
- Remaining calm when separated from owner
- Dogs passing the test can receive a CGC certificate and tag from the AKC. For information on upcoming tests, visit the AKC website.

ditions. Dogs must demonstrate the ability to tolerate gunfire, retrieve game from water, take direction, and return retrieved birds to a handler. Unlike field trials, hunt tests are noncompetitive. Each dog's performance is judged against an established standard of perfection. Poodles can compete for three successively more difficult titles: Junior Hunter (JH), Senior Hunter (SH), and Master Hunter (MH).

The first Poodle to earn a Master Hunter title was HR Ch. CCh Bibelot's Silver Power Play UD MH WCX, known as Pie. At 18 months of age, Pie appeared at an AKC hunt test as a demo dog. Then CDX titled, he was the only dog at that test to complete a blind retrieve without being redirected by his handler. He subsequently earned his UD and MH titles.

Poodles can also earn Poodle Club of America Working Certificates (WC) by completing land and water retrieves in approved field tests, completing a Working Certificate test or Working Certificate Excellent (WCX) test offered by an approved retriever club, or completing a hunt test of equal or greater difficulty held by an approved hunt club.

Hunting
Hunt tests and field trials evaluate instincts and skill in a simulated hunting environment. However, they can never re-create the unpredictable conditions of an actual hunt. Most Poodles will instinctively chase birds and dive

into water, but training is needed to refine these skills. More important, training improves your ability to read your dog and communicate effectively, strengthening your bond with your Poodle. Unlike some retrievers, many Poodles refuse to work with anyone other than the person they are accustomed to working with. Training a hunting Poodle is a serious commitment.

If this sounds like your cup of tea, improve your odds of success by training the right dog. Choose a puppy from hunting lines with pronounced natural instincts. He should willingly chase and retrieve, and demonstrate interest in birds. Postpone serious training until he is six months old. Younger puppies should have basic obedience training supplemented with hikes in the woods to explore, stalk birds, and build prey drive. During these walks, frequently encourage your puppy to come when called and pay attention when asked. This is critical groundwork to build his focus and self-control.

It's also important to interrupt and redirect him if he begins to develop bad habits, like hunting by scent rather than visually searching for game, or running himself to exhaustion in wild pursuit. He must learn to be attentive to his environment in order to perform blind retrieves and navigate the normal hazards of retrieving work without injury. This balance of caution and confidence is known as terrain courage.

Obviously, you have plenty of work to do before your Poodle is ready for training at six months. You'll also need to use this time to find and join a retriever club. The club will give you access to expert advice, friends to train with, and a range of training sites to familiarize your Poodle with different terrain and conditions.

Other Sports

If you prefer less traditional sports, there are plenty of choices sure to appeal to Poodles.

Flyball If your Poodle is addicted to tennis balls, flyball may be his calling. Flyball was invented in the late 1960s by a group of California dog trainers attempting to combine scent training and hurdle racing into a single sport. The invention of the automatic tennis ball launcher or flyball box was the pivotal event that popularized the sport. The first flyball tournament took place in 1983, and the North American Flyball Association was founded in 1984. There are now over 400 flyball clubs in the United States sponsoring more than over 300 tournaments each year.

In competition, two teams of four dogs face off in a test of speed. Each dog races a 51-foot course, jumping four hurdles, triggering the flyball box, catching the ball, and returning to release the next dog in the relay. Most teams actively recruit small dogs, known as height dogs, because the hurdle height is set for the smallest dog on the team.

Disc Dog If your Poodle loves to leap and catch, Disc Dog might be his dream sport. Poodles of every size can participate, and the sport requires no equipment aside from a disc, a dog, and a backyard or park.

For as long as humans have tossed Frisbees, dogs have joined in. The canine version of this pastime traces its origin to a legendary 1974 baseball

game at Dodger Stadium. College student Alex Stein ran onto the field with his dog, Ashley Whippet, to demonstrate the sport for a national TV audience. Since then, it has grown from a backyard pastime into an organized international sport. Several Disc Dog organizations sponsor amateur and professional tournaments with classes for dogs of every size and skill level.

Dock Diving If your Poodle is a true water dog, he will probably love dock diving. Since its introduction in 2000, dock diving has been refined into several competitive events to test speed, distance, and training.

- Big Air competition measures the distance of a dog's jump from the edge of a 40-foot dock to the base of the dog's tail where he lands in the water.
- Extreme Vertical measures the height of a dog's jump as he attempts to grab a toy suspended over a pool.
- Speed Retrieve is a timed race. From a starting line on the dock, dogs jump into the water and race to retrieve an artificial duck.
- Catch It is the most difficult Dock Diving event, combining distance jumping and retrieving.

Therapy Dog Programs

If you want a more meaningful career for your Poodle, consider training him for therapy work. Therapy dogs visit hospitals, nursing homes, rehabilitation centers, and hospices, where a little Poodle therapy is always welcome. These visits are especially beneficial for patients who are lonely, withdrawn, depressed, and missing their own pets.

Poodles are naturally affectionate and comforting. Their coat can also be tolerated by many individuals suffering from allergies or respiratory ailments. Several national therapy dog organizations provide evaluation and training for dogs and handlers interested in this field. Dogs must be familiar with basic obedience and pass a Canine Good Citizen test prior to being accepted for therapy dog training.

Travel Safety

Sports usually involve traveling to competitions, and your Poodle should be familiarized with travel during his socialization period. Begin with short car trips. Inexperienced dogs should travel on an empty stomach to offset possible motion sickness. If your Poodle suffers severe travel sickness, consult your veterinarian about medications to alleviate symptoms.

Always crate your dog while driving. Crates should be secured on a flat surface to prevent sliding and bouncing around the car. Wire crates provide better ventilation and may minimize motion sickness because the dog has a clear view of his surroundings. For air travel, an airline-approved plastic or aluminum crate is required.

When traveling by plane, your Poodle will also need a veterinarian's health certificate. However, pet travel requirements change frequently and vary according to destination. Regulations and policies also vary between airlines. For instance, most airlines limit the number of pets per flight, and many international flights don't permit any pets to travel in the cabin. If your Poodle must travel in the cargo hold, research the airline's pet safety record, book a direct flight, and avoid traveling during extreme weather, major holidays, or weekends, when planes are more likely to be delayed, grounded, or rerouted.

CHECKLIST

Travel Supplies

Cleaning
✔ Paper towels
✔ Pre-moistened disinfectant wipes
✔ Aerosol room deodorizer
✔ Plastic bags in case of accidents

Nutrition
✔ Stick to your dog's normal feeding and exercise schedule
✔ Make sure he drinks enough water, especially in the hot weather
✔ Bottled water

First aid
✔ If your dog needs prescription drugs, carry a back-up supply in case of lost luggage
✔ Hot and cold packs
✔ Thermometer
✔ Penlight

✔ Self-sticking bandages
✔ First aid tape
✔ Gauze (can also be used for a makeshift muzzle)
✔ Scissors
✔ Tweezers
✔ Over-the-counter medications for vomiting and diarrhea
✔ Ointments for minor wounds and skin irritations
✔ Peroxide or disinfectant solution to clean wounds
✔ Oral glucose solution
✔ Syringe to administer liquid medications
✔ Splinting materials, such as plastic spoon, paint stick, or ruler
✔ Sterile eye wash or artificial tears
✔ Benadryl to counteract allergic reactions

Airlines won't accept sedated animals, so your Poodle should be trained to remain calmly in his carrier. He should be lightly fed and exercised before the flight. Remove his collar, and line the crate with absorbent bedding in case of an accident. Dishes must be anchored to the door; water dishes should be filled with ice to prevent spilling. Supplement airline stickers with labels stating your flight number, dog's name and breed, and contact information at home and at your destination. Also attach labels stating that the crate should not be opened, and secure the door with zip ties after the security inspection. After boarding, confirm that your dog is loaded onto the plane, and find out exactly where and when pets can be picked up on arrival.

If your dog is traveling in the cabin you will need to remove him from his carrier for security screening prior to boarding. Have a leash ready. Even well-trained dogs may become panicky and confused. After the flight, do not let him out of the crate until you are in a secure area. Always attach his leash before letting him out.

If you will be staying at a hotel, make sure you have all the information to provide a safe and happy stay for you and your poodle. Some hotels require a security deposit, limit the number of pets per room, or require dogs to be crated. Check if the hotel has a designated dog exercise area, and always clean up after your dog.

Leash Training

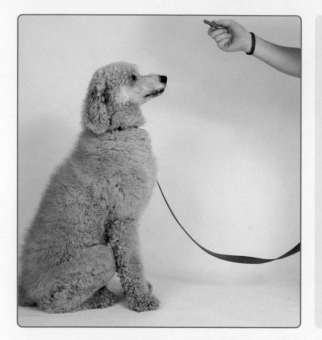

1 Pick up the leash, call his name, show him that you have a treat, and encourage him to follow you. If he hesitates, be patient. Never pull to get him moving. If he lunges to the end of the lead and begins pulling, stop. If he gets what he wants by pulling, it will become his habit.

2 Whenever he keeps pace with you, tell him *"Heel"* and reward him with praise and a treat. A clicker can also be used to reinforce this idea while he is walking at your side. Click/treat when he walks calmly at a nice pace. Slight tension in the lead helps him to sense your speed and anticipate your stops and turns. The leash should never be taut or loose.

3 Stop immediately if the leash becomes taut due to his lagging or pulling. Use treats and praise to lure him back to your side, and continue reinforcing the idea that walking at your pace earns rewards. He will choose to walk at your side if he understands this. You can also practice the *heel* command off lead in a small, safe, enclosed area.

4 When he understands *heel*, add an additional command like *go ahead* to let him know when it is okay to run to the end of the lead to sniff and investigate. However, he should never be permitted to pull or drag you if something catches his fancy. If you consistently stop and tell him *"Heel"* when this happens, he will never develop the habit of forging ahead. Do not underestimate his ability to sense the correct tension on the lead.

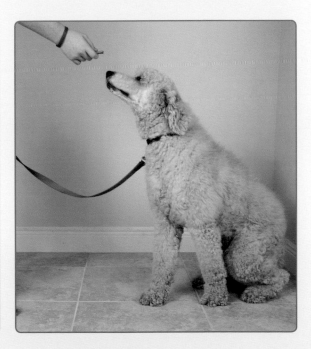

121

The Sit Command

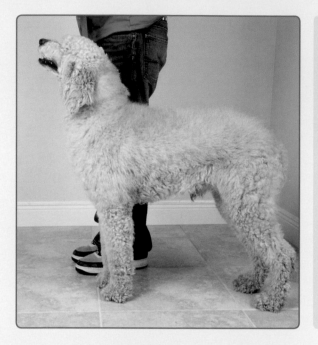

1 Call him to you. When he is standing a few inches in front of you, show him the treat in your hand.

2 Hold the treat just above his nose and wait. If he tries to jump or grab it, close your fist to prevent this, but don't move. If you start dodging him, he will get excited and think it's a game. You want him to relax.

3 In order to remain comfortable while watching the treat, he will eventually sit. Be patient. As soon as he does this, tell him *"Sit,"* and give him the treat.

4 Follow up with a unique release command like "okay" or "good boy" to signal when he should get up. As his performance improves, wait a few seconds before releasing him. With practice, he should be able to sit calmly for one minute.

The Stay Command

1 Attach his leash and call his name to get his attention. Use a treat to lure him to your side, and tell him *"sit."*

2 After a few seconds step around to face him. Make eye contact, take a few steps backward, and tell him *"Stay."*

3 Maintain eye contact to encourage him to remain still. Watch his body posture. If he begins to shift his weight, or get up and walk off, interrupt him. Put him back into the *sit* position and repeat the *stay* command.

4 After he remains sitting for a minute, give a unique release command, call him to you, and reward him. Do not use the same word to signal his release from *sit* and *stay*, as this may confuse him.

Chapter Eight

Grooming

Regular brushing and periodic trimming are essential to ensure your Poodle's health and comfort. He will be prone to numerous ailments if his coat is matted, ears dirty, nails overgrown, and teeth covered in tartar. And don't overlook the psychological impact of neglected grooming. Your dog will not feel healthy, comfortable, or wanted. You will find him less appealing and consequently, spend less time around him. A clean dog also makes for a clean home. Although Poodles don't shed, curly coats are dirt magnets. Your floors, walls, and furniture will become a reflection of your grimy pet and sloppy grooming, and will further undermine your relationship with him. Grooming is a demonstration of the value you place in your dog, and he will recognize this.

Tools and Equipment

Combs and brushes from the dog food isle of the grocery store are economical, but they cost more than good-quality ones in the long run. They wear out quickly, they don't do a thorough job, and they cause coat damage that encourages matting. You will pay more for equipment from retailers specializing in top-of-the-line grooming tools, but this is a worthwhile investment.

Poodle care is labor intensive, and frequent grooming is the only way to minimize this workload. Groom your Poodle consistently and you will not face tedious tasks like dematting.

You are less likely to accidentally trim a nail too short if you trim his nails regularly. His skin will be less sensitive and prone to clipper rash if he is clipped frequently. Most of all, he will learn to accept this as a daily part of his life, and grooming will never turn into a stressful confrontation.

If your Poodle doesn't need daily brushing, alternate grooming chores like teeth cleaning, nail trimming, and brushing. Every session, place him on a table for a two-minute exam to check for rashes, fleas, mats, injuries, and general body condition.

Puppies should be familiarized with grooming from eight weeks of age, including bathing, blow drying, nail trimming, and clipping. At this age, daily practice is essential to accustom your Poodle to each aspect of grooming that will become part of his adult life. He should be trained to stand and lie on a table. Without his cooperation, it will be impossible to completely brush his coat. Use specific commands to let him know when to lie on his side, turn around, and hold still for detail work.

CHECKLIST

Poodle Grooming Tools

✔ A slicker brush for thick coats

✔ A pin brush (without balls on the tips of the pins) for brushing longer portions of the coat

✔ A steel comb with rounded teeth, half fine-spaced, half medium-spaced. (Teeth should be 1½ inches [3.8 cm] long for Standards, 1 inch [2.5 cm] long for Miniatures, and ¾ inch [1.9 cm] long for Toys to ensure that they penetrate completely through the coat to the skin.)

✔ Stainless steel scissors, both straight and curved (7-inch [17.8 cm] for Toys and Miniatures, 8–10 inch [20–25 cm] for Standards)

✔ Blunt-tipped scissors

✔ Guillotine-type nail trimmer or nail grinder

✔ Styptic powder

✔ Ear cleaning solution and ear powder

✔ Hemostat or tweezers to remove excess hair from ear canals

✔ Doggy toothpaste and toothbrush or gauze pads for dental cleaning

✔ Coat conditioning spray

✔ Detangling spray

✔ pH-balanced shampoo and conditioner for harsh coats

✔ Grooming table or similar nonskid surface

✔ Grooming arm and noose (optional)

✔ Hair dryer

✔ Clamp to attach a handheld dryer to a table (optional) (Drying time will be shorter if you invest in a forced-air dryer or a stand dryer.)

✔ Electric clipper, blades, and accessories to maintain blades and clipper

Even if you plan to have your Poodle professionally groomed, you will need a convenient grooming workstation at home. It can be in your kitchen, basement, laundry room, or anywhere with an available sink or tub for dog bathing. It should be draft-free, with good lighting, storage space, and access to electric outlets. Toys and Minis can be placed on a table for grooming, but you may want to train your Standard to hop up. Use a treat to lure him up, giving a command like *jump* or *table* when he does. Use the *stay* command to keep him there. A grooming arm and noose will help to keep him still during grooming, but you should never leave him unattended in a grooming noose.

Brushing

Because Poodles don't shed, dead hair must be brushed out to prevent matting. Coat length, texture, and trim will dictate whether a pin brush or a wire slicker is the best choice for routine brushing. Both can be effective or useless. Test brushes by trying them yourself. A cheaply made brush is stiff

and sharp. It will rip hair and damage skin. A sharp brush can also cause skin irritation known as brush burn.

Puppy coats range from slightly wavy to tightly curled. Weekly brushing is fine for many puppies, but soft, cottony coats require more frequent attention to prevent mats. Coat change occurs between 7 and 18 months of age, and many Poodles will need daily brushing for several months as the puppy coat is gradually shed and replaced. The amount of brushing needed for adult coats also varies. The only rule is that the dog should be kept free of mats.

Brush methodically, one section at a time. Do each leg, his tail, topknot, ears, and body coat. Longer, dense coats should be parted into sections about 2 or 3 inches wide and misted with conditioning spray to reduce static. Brush gently from the hair tips to the roots, all the way to the skin in a smooth motion, without bending your wrist. After brushing, use your comb to check for tiny tangles that you may have missed. They have a miraculous ability to triple in size by the next grooming session.

Helpful Hints

Bath accessories—like bathing nooses, spray attachments for rinsing, and ramps to help large dogs get into the bath—can be purchased through pet supply catalogs.

Bathing

Dirty hair is more prone to matting. Poodles should be bathed every three to four weeks, but puppies may need weekly bathing to keep them clean and free of mats until their coat change is complete. Never bathe a matted coat. The mats will tighten, making them impossible to remove.

Smaller Poodles can be bathed in a kitchen or laundry sink. Standards will need to go into a regular-sized tub. Place a nonskid mat in the bottom. If necessary, secure him with a noose before you start, as dogs can be injured jumping out of the bath. Thoroughly wet his coat and gently lather the shampoo. Be careful not to get it into his eyes or scrub it into his coat, which can cause mats. Rinse thoroughly from head to tail. Soap residue in his coat can cause skin irritation and matting. If you apply a conditioner, pay special attention to areas prone to matting, such as the neck, sides, and under the front legs. Leave the conditioner on for several minutes before rinsing.

Drying

Towel dry the coat gently to sop up moisture, but do not rub. If the weather is warm and his coat is short, you can allow him to air dry. However, this will leave his coat much curlier and more prone to matting. For a straighter, fluffier finish, brush and stretch each section of the coat as it dries. This

requires two hands. If you don't have a stand dryer, a handheld dryer can be clamped to the table or grooming arm. Set it on medium, and check frequently to make sure it never becomes too hot. Pull each section of hair straight with your brush as you dry it. The rest of the coat should remain covered by a towel to keep it flat. Gradually uncover each section as you work on it. If part of the coat dries before you get to it, mist it with your sprayer. Double-check the ears, under the front legs, and other hard-to-reach spots for dampness. This is especially important if your Poodle has a soft, cottony coat. Damp hair will curl and clump, inviting mats.

Trimming

Professional grooming is one of the biggest expenses associated with this breed. Depending on your dog's coat quality, lifestyle, and trim, he should be clipped every four to eight weeks. Elderly dogs may require less, and puppies may need more frequent attention to keep up with new coat growth. You can minimize costs with a one-time investment in groom-

Breed Needs

Blade Guide

3F: ½-inch (1.5 cm) coat length

4F: ⅜-inch (1 cm) coat length

5F: ¼-inch (.6 cm) coat length

7F: ⅛-inch (.3 cm) coat length

ing tools and learn to groom your dog yourself. Books and videos can get you started, but you will also need hands-on mentoring. Ask your breeder for a grooming lesson or contact a local Poodle club for assistance. If you don't feel ready for that, you can economize to some extent by alternating visits to the groomer with regular coat maintenance at home.

Clippers

Clippers can seem intimidating, but once you learn the basics, they are an excellent tool to keep your Poodle's trim neat between visits to the groomer. The Oster A5 clipper has been the traditional choice for decades. In recent years, a wide range of lightweight cordless clippers and finishing trimmers have become available. These are comfortable to hold, quiet, easy to maneuver, and much less daunting for novice groomers.

You will need at least two blades. Higher numbers produce shorter trims. 3F (F stands for finish) 5F,

Helpful Hints

Clipper Facts

Never set your clippers on the table where your dog can knock them off. This is the most common way that clippers and blades are broken.

Clean and oil blades after each use. Remove debris with a small, stiff brush, and canned air. Apply one or two drops of oil between the blades. Dirty blades heat up quickly, jam frequently, and produce a lot of noise and vibration. If cleaning and oiling does not solve the problem, the blade needs sharpening.

Clipping a dirty coat will dull your blades, and dull blades will tear the coat.

Work slowly, in good light. Hold the blade parallel and flat against the coat. Be careful not to dig it into the skin. Use your fingers to stretch the skin taut and smooth as you clip, stopping to evaluate your work every few minutes.

and 7F are the favorite choices for the body coat. For his face, feet, and tail you will need a 10 or 15 blade. A 10 blade leaves the coat about 1/16th inch (.2 cm) long, and the 15, sometimes called a Poodle blade, produces a closer shave. Show trims are usually done with a 40 or 50 blade, which removes coat down to the skin. These blades are not recommended for inexperienced groomers. Skip tooth blades are also more likely to cause accidental nicks. Detachable plastic and stainless guide combs are available in many sizes. They can be snapped over clipper blades to ensure even coat length.

Scissors

Use your scissors to neaten up stray hairs and to blend longer and shorter portions of your Poodle's trim. Curved scissors are better for rounding off edges and shaping the coat to body contours. Hold the scissors with your thumb and ring finger. Use your index and middle fingers to support the blade, placing your pinky in the finger rest. You will have better control if you use just your thumb, instead of your entire hand, when cutting. Use the whole blade, rather than snipping at the coat with the tips of the blades.

Scissor parallel to the skin in a smooth, flowing motion. Always cut in the direction of the hair growth. Trim vertically from the top down, rather than horizontally, to prevent scissor marks in the coat. Comb and fluff each area of the coat as you scissor to ensure evenness. Work slowly and stop to evaluate the results frequently from different angles. It's easy to underestimate how much you are taking off. Evaluating your work in a mirror provides a much clearer picture of balance and symmetry. Uneven, crooked lines will appear magnified. Pay attention to what you are doing, but don't be intimidated. Scissoring requires confidence and a steady hand. You will make mistakes, but this is the only way to learn.

Continental or Town and Country?

Unlike most breeds, the Poodle has no standard Poodle trim. You can choose from a myriad of plain and fancy styles, each of which has particular advantages and disadvantages. Your choice should be based on your personal taste, your Poodle's lifestyle, the texture and density of his coat, and the amount of time and money you can devote to coat care. If he is basically an indoor dog, and you are prepared to maintain a fancy trim, choose something to delight the eye and show off his beauty. Longer, complicated trims require more maintenance grooming and frequent visits to the groomer. With a shorter, plain style, you may be able to get by with weekly brushing and professional grooming every two to three months. If your Poodle spends a lot of time outdoors, your budget is tight, or you lack confidence in your grooming skills, do him a favor and keep him in a short basic trim.

Professional groomers calculate prices based on the size of the dog, the complexity of the trim, and the dog's condition. Needles to say, grooming a well-maintained coat is far less work than tackling an overgrown, dirty, matted coat.

The typical price for a bath and complete grooming for a basic trim usually includes a clean face and feet, a shorter body coat, and slightly fuller legs. For Toys and Miniatures, $55–$75 is the norm, and for Standards, $100–$140 is typical.

Complicated styles like the town and country, with a full body and legs, generally cost $20–$50 more because of the time and work involved.

Breed Needs

Removing Mats

Some dogs seem to develop mats behind their ears, in their armpits, and inside their back legs, no matter how frequently they are brushed. Dematting always causes coat loss, but most mats will give way to patience and persistence. Saturate the mat with detangler, and use your fingers to pull it apart at the edges. Alternate this with teasing it apart with a slicker brush, and using one tooth of the comb to catch and untangle a few hairs. Repeat these steps until the mat comes apart. Remember, dematting is uncomfortable for the dog. Provide frequent breaks and plenty of praise throughout the process. If matting is extensive, it is more humane to sacrifice coat and use a mat splitter.

Poodle Trims

The AKC standard permits four Poodle trims, so options are limited for show dogs. However, there are a myriad of trim styles for pet Poodles. Some of these are widely popular, but, just as with show trims, that does not imply that groomers follow universally accepted patterns. If you request a particular style, don't assume

FYI: Cording a Coat

A harsh, thick, curly-textured coat will cord into long, rope-like mats without much assistance. Bathing the dog and allowing his coat to dry naturally is usually sufficient to start the process. Thinner, straighter coats require more work to produce cords of uniform length and thickness. Cording usually begins at around seven to nine months of age when the adult coat starts coming in. As the shed puppy coat becomes entangled with the emerging adult coat, the hair will fuse into bundles. Most of the work involves keeping each evolving cord separated as it becomes thicker and longer.

Some coats mat rather than cord naturally, and the mats must be manually separated into increasingly smaller sections by gently pulling them apart. The thickness of the cords should be in proportion to the size of the dog. Once they are established, the cords should be sprayed with water daily to tighten them and encourage the process. Corded Poodle coats have been known to grow to 20 inches.

A corded coat must be kept scrupulously clean and well conditioned. It should be bathed weekly in low-suds shampoo to prevent the build-up of soap residue. Use a light conditioner that is easily rinsed out. The coat must be thoroughly dried to prevent skin problems, which will take several hours. Dampness can also cause the cords to develop mildew and odor. Soaking the dog in a mixture of a teaspoon of chlorine bleach diluted in 5 gallons of water will stop cord mildew. The cords must be checked for debris like twigs, grass, and seeds each day, and protected from breakage. Their thickness is deceptive; only some of the hair is actually anchoring them to the skin, and they can be easily damaged or pulled out. Cords should be tied into bundles with hair scrunchies to protect them.

that a groomer will have exactly the same thing in mind. You may return to find that your dog's entire body coat has been removed if you don't specify a desired length. Be prepared with a precise description. If you want a mustache rather than a clean face, for example, it can be done in several ways: donut mustache and beard, sweetheart mustache and beard, or French mustache. Most professional groomers have photo books illustrating various styles and will offer suggestions.

Thanks to technical improvements in coat care and equipment, Poodle grooming has improved significantly in the past decade. Rather than simply following a pattern, styles can be individualized to enhance your dog's physical advantages and disguise his flaws. A trim should never create the illusion of imperfections that he doesn't possess. Your Poodle's coat texture and color will also affect the appearance of various trims. As you watch your Poodle, you may decide that he would look better with a little more hair here and a little less there. Trims can be subtly shaped and refined with judicious scissoring and trimming.

The Puppy Clip The AKC standard requires Poodles under a year old to be shown in a puppy trim. The coat on the body and legs is left long and shaped with scissors. The front legs are shaped into straight columns, and the rear legs are trimmed to follow the body contour. The coat on the neck is left full. The topknot is pulled into a ponytail. The face, throat, feet, and base of tail are shaved with a #15 or #10 blade. The pompon on the tail is shaped with scissors.

Dogs over one year old must be shown in the continental or English saddle, depending on which one is most flattering to the dog's balance and proportions.

Continental The continental, with its shaved hindquarters, is the most familiar Poodle trim. The face, throat, feet, and base of the tail are shaved. The body coat is shaved to approximately 1 inch behind the last rib. The hindquarters are shaved, except for two rosettes on the hips. These are actually optional, but this detail is rarely omitted from the trim. The legs are shaved, leaving bracelets over the hocks and puffs at the pastern joint, which are shaped with scissors. The tail coat is shaped into a rounded pompon. The remainder of the body is fully coated and shaped with scissors to enhance proportions. The topknot is long and held off the face with a series of elastic bands.

English Saddle The English saddle involves much more trimming and scissoring. It is considered the most technically challenging Poodle trim, which explains why it is not often seen in the show ring. The body coat is full and shaped. The forelegs are shaved, leaving puffs at the pasterns, which are shaped with scissors. The coat on the hindquarters is scissored shorter into a smooth blanket, with two crescent-shaped areas shaved onto the flanks. Two bands are shaved onto each hindleg. The face, throat, base of the tail, and feet are shaved. The topknot is long and pulled into a ponytail with elastic bands, and a rounded pompon is scissored onto the tail.

Sporting Trim Poodles exhibited in non-regular classes can be shown in a sporting trim, which requires much less regular maintenance. Also called a kennel trim, this is a shorter version of the puppy trim. The neck and body coat is trimmed to no more than 1 inch long. The leg coat is left slightly longer. The body and legs are scissored to follow natural contours. The face, feet, throat, and base of the tail are shaved. The topknot is scissored into a rounded cap to balance the size of the pompon covering the tail.

Retriever Trim The retriever trim is a shorter version of the sporting trim. The body and legs are trimmed uniformly short. The face, feet, throat, and base of the tail are shaved. The topknot is shaped into a rounded cap, and no pompon is left on the tail.

Working Continental This is a shorter version of the continental, similar to a traditional hunting trim. It is somewhat less complicated than the full version. It preserves the typical Poodle silhouette while providing protection from the elements. The legs, tail, and hindquarters are trimmed to 1–2 inches following the pattern of the continental but omitting the rosettes. Scissors are used to shorten and shape the topknot, mane, and remainder of the body coat to a manageable length. Bracelets, puffs, and pompon are shaped tighter than the traditional version. The face and feet are shaved.

Lamb Trim The lamb trim is the most popular style for pet Poodles today. It is easy to maintain but provides enough coat length to look stylish and disguise faults. The body coat is trimmed to a length specified by the owner. The legs are left slightly longer and fluffier. The front legs are scissored into columns, with the hind legs trimmed to follow body contours. The face, feet, and base of the tail are shaved. The pompon on the tail is shaped round or oval. The topknot is scissored short to balance the pompon on the tail.

Clown Trim The clown, bikini, ponjola, Miami, and summer trim are all variations of the same style. Basically, the feet and base of the tail are shaved closely. The body coat is trimmed short and fluffy. The leg coat is trimmed close with modified puffs and bracelets shaped onto the legs at the hock and pastern joints.

Fancy Pet Trims Once popular, the town and country and Dutch trims have lost favor with both groomers and owners because they require painstaking, detailed clipping, hand scissoring, extensive maintenance, and frequent trips to the groomer.

Dutch Trim The Dutch or royal Dutch trim was actually invented in France. The body coat is clipped short on the neck, throat, chest, abdomen, and the back, from the top of the neck to the base of the tail. The coat is left full on the legs and trimmed into an oval shape above the shoulders and hips. The feet and base of the tail are shaved. The coat on the ears is trimmed short except for fringe at the bottom. The topknot is rounded off. The face is shaved except for a mustache at the end of the muzzle.

Town and Country The face, neck, feet, base of the tail, and a wide belly band are shaved closely. Lines are shaved between the shoulders and hips along the back, into the belly band. The rest of the coat is left long and fluffy, and shaped with hand scissoring.

CAUTION

Preventing and Treating Clipper Burn

Light-colored Poodles and dogs that are trimmed infrequently have more sensitive skin, making them more prone to clipper burn.

Always work on a freshly bathed coat and use good-quality clippers with sharp blades. Forcing a dull blade through the coat will cause clipper burn.

If you are inexperienced, avoid using #30 blades and higher. These are more likely to cause clipper burn if you are not skillful.

High-speed clippers heat up faster and hot blades can cause clipper burn. Check the blade frequently while you work. If it begins to heat up, change blades or stop until the blade cools down. Coolant spray can also help to keep blades cool and lubricated. Wipe off residue before use.

Clipper rash usually heals in three days. It should be treated with topical antibiotic, cortisone cream, or diaper rash ointment. Keep the injury clean and prevent the dog from scratching it, which can lead to secondary infections.

Grooming Tips

Feet

Shaved feet look neat and minimize the dirt tracked into your house. With a little practice, you can learn to touch up your Poodle's feet in between visits to the groomer.

Use a #10 or #15 blade, and shave against the direction of hair growth beginning at the base of the nails. If your Poodle is in a pattern, use this as a guide. Do not shave higher than the end of the big pad on the back of the foot. Shave all the hair from the top, spread the toes with your free hand, and carefully remove hair between them.

Ears

Poodles should have their ears checked daily and rinsed weekly with ear cleaning solution or a mild dilution of water and vinegar. Regular cleaning maintains a pH level that will discourage infection. Hold the ear flap open, squeeze the solution into the ear canal, massage it in, and wipe away any debris with a cotton ball. His ear leather and ear canal should be pale pink, dry, and odorless. Head shaking, ear scratching, redness, or noticeable odor merit a trip to the veterinarian.

Ear mites, burrs, and foxtails in the ear canal are not visible, but they will cause severe pain and ongoing trouble. Dampness invites infection, and yeast and bacterial infections are common causes of canine ear trouble. Ears must be thoroughly dried after a bath or swim. Use a handheld dryer on low to dry them inside and out.

Keeping his ear canals free of hair also helps prevent a build-up of debris and bacteria. Sprinkle ear powder or baking soda onto the hair to make it easy to grip. Gently pull with your fingertips or tweezers, and it should come out easily and painlessly. Hair growing on the ear flap or around the base of the ear is not easily removed, and trying to do so will cause pain.

Topknots

Hair falling into your dog's eyes is uncomfortable and unsanitary. Your Poodle's head coat must be trimmed or banded into a topknot. To scissor the topknot, comb all the hair over to one side. Trim with curved scissors following the outline of the head from the eye over the ear, stopping just behind the ear. Comb the hair to the other side and scissor the same line again. Continue combing and shaping until it is symmetrical.

If it is not trimmed, his head coat will be long enough to band by six months of age. He should be accustomed to wearing topknot bands earlier to ensure that he does not yank or chew them off and destroy his head coat. By three or four months of age, begin putting a barrette or orthodontic band in his topknot during his daily grooming session. At first, he will do his best to remove it. Just keep putting it back until he becomes accustomed to it. This won't cause much damage to a short puppy coat.

Comb up the hair from the bridge of his muzzle to the outside corners of his eyes, being careful not catch his ear coat or pull the hair too tightly. Wrap a band twice around the hair to secure it. It should be brushed out and redone every couple of days. Cut the band with blunt-tipped scissors to remove it, never pull it out. Add additional bands every 2 or 3 inches as his coat grows.

Controlling Eye Stains

Tears contain proteins that can cause discoloration beneath the eyes. When the dog produces tears faster than the tear ducts absorb them, the remainder will overflow, causing wetness and reddish discoloration. Most eye staining can be controlled by daily cleaning with a damp cotton ball or baby wipe. It's also helpful to keep the hair shaved closely on his face and pat corn-starch around the area to keep it dry. It may also help to dab waterproof ointment, like petroleum jelly, under the eyes to repel moisture.

Dogs with very large eyes and short muzzles are more prone to tear staining. It can also occur in dogs with small tear ducts and watery eyes. Wind, dust, pollen, tiny injuries, and allergies are other common reasons for watery eyes. Daily eyewash can help to rinse away environmental irri-tations. If you suspect a dust or pollen allergy, ionizers and air filters can be used to lower the allergen levels in your home. Keeping your Poodle indoors when the pollen count is high may also help.

Very dark tear stains that appear suddenly may be triggered by an allergy to a food, supplement, additive, grooming product, or water with a high mineral content. Switching to an additive-free food or bottled water may

BE PREPARED! Foot Care and Nail Trimming

Every dog must have his nails clipped, and every Poodle trim includes shaving the feet. Puppies should become accustomed to having their feet handled. Ideally nails should be trimmed weekly, so it's preferable to learn to do this yourself, rather than waiting for monthly or bimonthly trips to the groomer. Yes, accidents can happen, and trimming a nail too short will hurt. However, this is not the reason why dogs become phobic about having their feet handled or nails trimmed. Use plenty of positive reinforcement when introducing your Poodle to nail trimming. Work slowly and provide frequent reassurance and rewards. Never become impatient or confrontational. This almost guarantees that your Poodle will fear the chore.

Nails are made of three layers. The hard outer shell and middle layer are insensitive. Only the center layer contains live tissue, known as the quick. The quick does not extend the entire length of the nail, and trimming the nail tips causes no discomfort for the dog. If his nails are maintained at a short length, the quick will recede, lessening the possibility of accidental injury.

To begin, have him stand or sit on a table. Grasp his foot firmly, slightly spread his toes apart, and snip the pointed tip off the nail. Tell him he's a good boy, give him a treat, and proceed to the next nail. If necessary, go through the motions daily until he is relaxed and comfortable about nail trimming. An uncooperative, struggling dog is much more likely to end up with a short nail, or a nick from the clipper. Accidents like this will reinforce his existing fears, leading to a vicious cycle.

A short nail is painful and will bleed, but it is not a serious injury. Styptic powder, or pressure and ice, will stop the bleeding. Do not hold the foot under running water, and do not allow him to walk on it until you are certain the bleeding has stopped. Nails are softer and more pliable after a bath, which can make trimming easier.

Nail Grinding

A grinder can also be used to keep nails short. Use either a low-rpm (5,000 to 10,000 rpm) cordless Dremel nail grinder or an Oster nail grinder, which is lighter and easier to use on small dogs.

Start with positive reinforcement to introduce your Poodle to the sound and vibration of the grinder before using it on his nails. Press your thumb against the footpad to spread the toes and lightly touch the rotating grinder wheel to the nail tip. Do not apply pressure. Repeat until the nail is the desired length.

help. Dental problems and ear infections can also cause excessive tearing. It is not unusual for puppies to develop tear staining during teething.

Consult your veterinarian if your Poodle suffers from serious, chronic tear staining. Surgery to enlarge tear ducts is rarely recommended. Most commonly, a combination of eye drops and a broad-spectrum antibiotic will be prescribed for a period of three weeks. Antibiotic therapy typically shows results in three weeks.

Chapter Nine

The Senior Poodle

Poodles are like a fine wine; they only improve with age. As the years go by, you will value your Poodle's companionship more and more, and find it hard to imagine life without him. Thankfully, Poodles are noted for their longevity. Miniature and Toy Poodles usually begin to slow down around age 12 and typically live to be 15 to 18. A few have lived to 20. The Standard Poodle's life span ranges from 10 to 13 years, and signs of aging normally begin to appear between nine and ten. Thanks to improvements in routine care, dogs no longer contend with factors that formerly shortened their lives, like infectious disease, chronic parasite infestation, and nutritional deficiencies. In the past, geriatric health issues received little or no veterinary attention simply because few dogs lived long enough to develop them.

The good news is that research on human aging has led to discoveries and innovations that are equally applicable to canine geriatric care. We can now manage age-related disorders that were formerly unrecognized or considered untreatable. We also have a much better understanding of how to ensure continued quality of life for our senior dogs. You cannot stop the aging process, but your senior Poodles can certainly enjoy a happy and comfortable old age.

As your Poodle gets older he may become less responsive, slower to react to commands, easily startled, confused, or less interested in his surroundings. Many behavior changes are the result of deteriorating senses. He may lose vision as his lenses and corneas cloud. Hearing loss usually starts with dwindling ability to hear high-pitched sounds. His sense of taste may also dull, and his appetite may suffer as a result. The canine olfactory sense is the most impervious to the effects of old age. Dogs rely on this sense more than any other, which helps them cope with the deterioration of other senses. Poodles adjust so well to these changes that you may not even realize he is experiencing sensory problems.

Modifying a Senior Dog's Environment

Dogs normally dislike major changes in their routines, and this tendency becomes more pronounced as they get older. Think carefully before revising your Poodle's customary food, exercise schedule, or grooming routine.

Changes can be especially challenging if he is coping with deteriorating hearing or sight. Familiar aspects of his routine provide a sense of comfort and security, reassuring him that he can capably function as part of your pack.

However, some modifications may be needed to ensure his continued health, comfort, and safety.

If he has trouble climbing stairs or jumping on and off furniture, he may need a ramp or doggy steps. If his balance and footing are questionable, you may need to install baby gates across stairways, place nonskid mats on slippery floors, and block his access to potential hazards like swimming pools and decks.

Older dogs are less tolerant of temperature extremes. Make sure his bed is away from drafts and well padded with cushions and blankets. If he is suffering from degenerative joint disease or back problems, he may benefit from sleeping on an orthopedic mattress. He should be more closely monitored outdoors. He may be long past the days of making a mad dash out of an open gate, but confused, elderly dogs often wander off and become lost.

Breed Truths

The width and shape of a dog's foreleg is the barometer of canine bone density. Sturdy bones are strong and resilient, regardless of the dog's size. Muscle wasting is most readily apparent in a dog's rear legs. The back legs are designed to generate energy rather than bear weight. They should comfortably support about one third of his body weight. Dogs don't require a tremendous amount of exercise to maintain strong hindquarters. Simply running around the house will keep a Toy in fair condition. However, if he becomes reluctant to exercise due to joint or back problems, it will quickly show in his hindquarters. His hip bones will become more prominent as he loses pelvic muscle mass, and his thighs will become thin and flattened rather than defined and rounded. Walking up stairs or on a sandy beach will provide excellent exercise to strengthen back legs.

The Importance of Exercise

Poodles have a knack for fitting comfortably into a routine. This makes it easy to overlook an older dog's sedentary habits. Maintaining a senior dog's motivation to exercise regularly can be challenging. Without encouragement, he may easily give up this habit. Deteriorating muscle mass will also discourage his desire to exercise, which will hasten muscle atrophy along with bone density and joint integrity. As movement becomes more difficult and painful, he will become more sedentary. His balance and coordination will deteriorate, making him even more reluctant to exercise. This becomes a self-perpetuating cycle.

Exercise will also satisfy his ongoing need for mental stimulation. Poodles are working dogs, and you are not doing your old dog any favors by letting him retire to become a couch potato. Challenges not only provide crucial mental stimulation, they reassure him that he is needed.

BE PREPARED! Does Your Senior Poodle Need a Canine Companion?

A puppy can revitalize an older dog by providing social interaction and motivation to exercise. Twenty minutes of dog play provides an excellent workout. However, do not assume that every senior Poodle will welcome the arrival of a little friend. If you are considering acquiring a new puppy, do it while your Poodle is healthy enough to easily cope with this change. If he has been an only dog for many years, a new addition may cause stress and resentment.

The arrival of a new dog should not impact his normal routine or his daily individual attention. Reassure him that he is still top dog. Don't force him to interact with the puppy. He will do this when he is ready. Do not allow the puppy to tease him or take his things. Ensure that he has a quiet place to retreat for downtime. When the puppy reaches adolescence, watch carefully and be prepared to step in before any signs of bullying or confrontation happen.

Activities like hikes to look for birds, a refresher course in basic obedience, or accompanying you on daily errands can provide much-needed mental diversion.

Senior Poodles usually require modifications to their exercise habits. Some dogs demonstrate markedly less inclination for their former pastimes. If daily exercise has not been an integral part of his daily routine, he's less likely to demand it. If he normally looks forward to exercise each day, you

should be concerned if the suggestion of a walk or a game no longer triggers enthusiasm. Sudden disinterest may indicate sensory deterioration, chronic pain, or a subclinical health problem. If his veterinarian finds no underlying medical condition to prevent him from exercising, you need to take charge as his coach.

Many Poodles try to maintain their youthful pace despite physical limitations. This is especially true if your Poodle normally participated in one or more sports. He will not forget this enjoyment. Suddenly eliminating an important part of his daily routine might give his bones and muscles needed rest, but it will also have a serious negative impact on his mental health. If running and jumping leaves him stiff and sore the next day, implement a less taxing routine.

Getting Back into the Exercise Habit

Moderate regular exercise will forestall muscle atrophy, cartilage deterioration, and joint damage. If your Poodle has gotten out of the exercise habit, get your veterinarian's okay before starting a routine. Stick to slow-paced activities like

CAUTION

A muscle strain may require three to six weeks to heal. A tendon injury is more serious and may require more than eight weeks to heal. A damaged ligament may require surgical repair.

walks and don't be tempted to overdo it. Two or three short walks are far more beneficial than a marathon hike. Monitor his energy and stress levels during exercise sessions, and be ready to cut it short if you see indications of limping, stress, or exhaustion. Dogs live in the moment, and they are very good at concealing injuries. A slight muscle strain can become much worse if it is not allowed to rest.

Give him a five-minute rubdown before each exercise session, followed by five to ten minutes of slow walking to gradually raise his heart rate and metabolism. After each exercise session, repeat these steps to ensure that his respiration rate and body temperature are normal. Gentle stretching and massage are also good ways to help him cool down after exercise.

Grooming

Older dogs usually require less grooming, but they value this attention even more. This remains one of his major links to you and a primary means of confirming his ongoing importance. By this age, your Poodle is well aware of when he looks good, and as the old saying goes, when you look good, you feel good. Regular grooming also helps you spot minor physical symptoms that may indicate a major health issue. Older dogs have less efficient immune function, and minor ear, skin, or dental problems can quickly turn serious.

Regular grooming is important, but some aspects of the routine may need to be modified as he ages. Keep grooming sessions short to avoid tiring him. Consider switching him to a shorter, less complicated trim, but don't forego regular brushing. As his skin becomes drier and more fragile, less bathing and more brushing is the best approach. Frequent brushing stimulates oil glands and distributes oils through his coat. Use a light touch and a softer brush, and switch to a milder shampoo and moisturizing coat conditioner.

As he becomes less active his nails will not be subjected to wear from regular exercise, and they will require more frequent trimming. Long nails are more prone to break, because they become more brittle as he ages. Short nails also help him to maintain sure footing on slippery surfaces.

Nutrition

Human and canine studies repeatedly confirm that obesity sets the stage for a multitude of health issues. Your Poodle might inevitably develop one or more age-related disorders, but obesity will certainly hasten their onset and severity. These commonly include arthritis, cardiovascular disease, cancer, and autoimmune-mediated disorders. Keeping your Poodle at his ideal weight becomes more challenging as he ages. Older dogs, especially if they are neutered, may need up to 25 percent fewer calories because of normal changes in metabolism and activity level. If he is doing well on his present diet, simply adjusting his portion size may be enough to prevent excess weight gain.

FYI: Prescription Diets

Prescription diets contain special ratios of basic nutrients, designed to influence body functions like blood pressure or glucose metabolism in order to treat disorders such as heart disease, kidney disease, food allergies, and diabetes. For example, prescription diets to combat food allergies contain unusual forms of protein, such as buffalo or rabbit meat, because they are less likely to trigger an allergic reaction. Prescription diets are only available through veterinarians and should only be used under veterinary supervision. Feeding them to a healthy dog will cause nutritional imbalances.

Every dog requires dietary fat to process fat-soluble vitamins, maintain skin and coat condition, and enhance the taste of his food. However, fat contains twice as many calories per gram as protein, and most commercial dog foods contain 7–12 percent fat. This may be fine for a normal, healthy dog but a lower-fat formula may be necessary for a senior Poodle.

If your senior Poodle needs a weight reduction diet, you can also try replacing part of his ration with cooked vegetables, which are low in calories and rich in vitamins and antioxidants. Good choices include well-cooked green beans, broccoli, sprouts, carrots, sweet potatoes, and squash. This is preferable to switching to a high-fiber weight reduction formula. Fiber will fill him up, but he may develop dietary deficiencies, as senior dogs do not process nutrients as efficiently.

Research on aging has emphasized the value of antioxidants to combat damage caused by free radicals. These unstable molecules are produced by physical processes like respiration and metabolism, as well as environmental factors like exposure to pollution. The body normally combats their harmful effects, but this process becomes less efficient as your dog ages. The resulting damage slows cell division, and accumulating cell damage leads to chronic diseases like cancer. Antioxidants enhance immune function, preventing and repairing the damage caused by circulating free radicals.

Although he may need fewer calories, your Poodle may need significantly more protein in order to maintain muscle mass. Older dogs synthesize protein less efficiently and may require a diet of 75 percent meat to prevent muscle wasting. Traditionally it was believed that older dogs should consume less protein to prevent kidney damage, and a low-protein diet is recommended for dogs suffering from a liver or kidney disease. For senior dogs in normal health, high-quality protein will help maintain muscle mass and body condition.

Needless to say, a prescription diet will do no good if your Poodle refuses to eat it. He may not appreciate having his usual diet changed to something less tasty. Other factors may also take the edge off of his normally healthy appetite. Chronic pain and inactivity will undermine appetite. Food may

seem less enticing because of a diminishing sense of taste. Age-related dental problems can make it difficult for him to chew and swallow. Skipping meals can quickly lead to additional health problems for senior dogs.

Try switching to a smaller kibble or softer food. His appetite may improve if his daily ration is divided into several meals per day. A spoonful of grated cheese, tuna fish, lean cooked beef, or chicken broth on top may also tempt his appetite.

Water

Older dogs may not drink enough, making them more prone to bladder infections, kidney stones, and electrolyte imbalance due to dehydration. Your senior Poodle should drink approximately 1 ounce of water per pound of body weight daily.

Age-Related Health Issues

Veterinarians have become increasingly conscious of the importance of geriatric care. Dogs age much faster than humans, and an annual checkup is the equivalent of you visiting a doctor every four years. More frequent health exams are recommended for senior Poodles. Veterinary checks every six months are recommended for Toys between ages 9 and 11, Minis over age nine, and Standards over age eight.

Obvious indications of a health problem—like loss of appetite, suspicious lumps, sudden lethargy or exercise intolerance, unusual weight loss, noisy labored breathing, or coughing—merit an immediate trip to the veterinarian. A wait-and-see approach can have disastrous consequences for a senior dog with limited physical resources. If your gut feeling tells you that something is amiss, don't hesitate to call your veterinarian and follow up. Subtle behavior changes are often the earliest indication of a health issue. He may seem confused, withdrawn, anxious, or just a bit off color, without any obvious symptoms.

The leading causes of death in senior dogs are heart failure, cancer, kidney disease, and liver disease. Cancer and cardiac disease are more common in Standards, and kidney disease is more prevalent in Miniatures and Toys. Many of these conditions are asymptomatic until they become fairly advanced. Regular health screenings are the only means of detecting them at an early treatable stage.

A geriatric health check normally includes a physical exam to check his weight, teeth, eyes, heart rate, blood pressure, and general condition, as well as a fecal exam to detect internal parasites. Blood tests may be recommended to detect early signs of anemia, infection, liver or kidney disease, metabolic disorders, or hormone imbalance. Urinalysis can help to detect changes in kidney function, the presence of bladder stones or infection, or the onset of diabetes or Cushing's disease. An electrocardiogram may be recommended to monitor heart function. If any aspect of your dog's condition raises concerns, your veterinarian may also recommend X-rays, ultrasound, CAT scan, skin scrapings, biopsies, or additional blood tests.

Canine Cognitive Dysfunction

Canine cognitive dysfunction is often described as a canine version of Alzheimer's disease. It is characterized by decreased awareness and responsiveness, as well as sudden changes in behavior patterns. Symptoms may begin to appear as early as age seven or eight. Approximately one quarter of dogs over age 11 develop some symptoms, and more than half of dogs showing one sign of the disease subsequently develop others within a year. Since Poodles are a very long-lived breed, they are at risk for this problem.

An afflicted dog may become disorientated in familiar environments, wandering aimlessly around the house or getting lost in the backyard. He may forget household rules and obedience commands, or suddenly begin having housetraining lapses. Other symptoms include chronic barking for no apparent reason and restless wandering during the night.

No definite cause of the disease has yet been determined. Research suggests that there is some correlation between mental decline and the accumulation of toxic free radicals. Reduced blood flow to the brain may also interfere with the normal transmission of electrical signals between the brain's neurotransmitters. Hormones may also play a role. Studies suggest that neutered males may be more prone to cognitive dysfunction, and estrogen may provide some protection against brain aging.

If you suspect that your Poodle is developing this disorder, begin with a veterinary exam to rule out other possible reasons for his behavioral changes,

BE PREPARED! Drug Therapy

Although they cannot be cured, many age-related disorders respond to drug therapy and can be medically managed for the duration of your Poodle's life. This isn't as simple as it sounds. Every dog responds slightly differently to standard doses of the same drug, and every drug has potential side effects. However, adverse reactions pose a bigger risk for senior dogs. Numerous factors—like decreased muscle mass and body fat, kidney or liver impairment, and changes in metabolism—will affect drug absorption rates and the body's ability to recover from the effects of drug toxicity. Recommended dosages are calibrated for normal, healthy dogs. Your senior Poodle may need a lower dosage or a slightly different dosing schedule.

Read package inserts to ensure you are aware of a drug's possible side effects, and do not exceed recommended doses. Don't hesitate to contact your veterinarian if you notice signs of an adverse reaction, such as sudden unusual behavior, lethargy, vomiting, or lack of appetite. Monitor your dog's liver and kidney function with periodic blood tests, as his drug reactions may change over time.

If your dog is taking more than one prescription drug, make sure there is no potential for drug interactions. Check with your veterinarian before giving any over-the-counter drugs, natural remedies, herbal supplements, or vitamins in combination with prescription medications. These can also interact with prescription drugs or render them ineffective.

such as failing sight or hearing, chronic pain, or metabolic or endocrine dysfunction. For example, diseases that cause metabolic dysfunction can produce behavior changes ranging from extreme lethargy to drastic changes in sleep patterns. Tumors or organ failure can also alter normal behavior.

If your Poodle is diagnosed with canine cognitive dysfunction, there are steps you can take to slow its progress. Provide a structured routine with plenty of environmental stimulation, such as walks, play, and social interaction, to encourage alertness. Boredom will speed disease progression. Discourage anxiety-fueled activities like pacing, panting, chronic barking, and nocturnal wandering. Give him a refresher course in sitting quietly at your side for five or ten minute intervals. If he is having housetraining issues, add more potty breaks to his schedule and ensure that he has easy access to his elimination area.

Your veternarian may recommend a prescription diet to improve cognitive function or dietary supplements containing antioxidants, vitamin E, vitamin C, selenium, beta carotene, and omega-3 fatty acids. In some cases anipryl (selegiline hydrochloride) is prescribed to improve the brain's dopamine transmission. It is FDA-approved to treat Parkinson's disease and Alzheimer's disease in humans and pituitary-dependent Cushing's in dogs.

Chapter Ten

Special Considerations

Secondhand Poodles

Adopting a rescue or shelter dog gives an unwanted dog a second chance. It is a very generous gesture. It also entails far more effort and responsibility than simply buying a dog from a breeder. It should never be done casually, impulsively, or out of a misguided desire to obtain a free Poodle. Information on the dog's former home, background, or lineage can provide clues about his health and behavior issues. However, in many cases, you will have little or no information to guide you when adopting a rescue.

You must be prepared to cope with a myriad of unexpected health and training issues. Reality television has fostered the idea that canine behavior problems can be instantly reformed. This is rarely true, but most unwanted habits can be revised through behavior modification as long as you are willing to invest the necessary time and effort. Depending on the problem, you may face weeks or months of retraining to eliminate an unwanted behavior and replace it with a new habit.

Begin with a veterinary checkup to rule out possible physical causes of behavior issues. If your dog's problem is a straightforward behavior issue, use the right approach. You need to accurately identify the motivations that underlie an unwanted behavior in order to successfully revise it. Most of all, you need to understand his current mental framework. If your Poodle has come from a situation where he experienced little socialization and no training, you cannot fault him for failing to understand the rules. He may not even be aware of the fact that human rules exist. You may face weeks of work in order to establish communication before you can begin training him.

Many owners assume that shy, nervous behavior is an indication of past mistreatment. While it's certainly possible, without information on the dog's past history, there is no way to confirm this suspicion. Fear of strangers can also be a response to inadequate socialization. Coddling and reassuring the

dog will reinforce his problem rather than revise it. He may actually need introductions and new experiences to conquer his fears of social interaction.

Perhaps he came from a commercial kennel where every aspect of his life was controlled. From your perspective, living as a house pet is a tremendous improvement. However, he may not easily adapt to this monumental change of lifestyle. Suddenly being expected to adapt to a household filled with an assortment of children, adults, and other pets may trigger unbearable stress. In a kennel situation, some of his behaviors were completely restricted. He may find it hard to accept the concept of going outside to run and play, or spontaneously approaching a stranger. Other parts of his life were subject to no regulation. He may have no concept of housetraining. Barking, jumping, and fighting over food may be second nature to him because these behaviors were never discouraged. Rather than reveling in his new lifestyle, he may become nervous and withdrawn. He may need a slow introduction in order to accept these changes.

Give him at least three weeks to settle into his new home. If he has been in a shelter for any length of time, his adjustment period may be even longer, as any existing personality issues become intensified in that high-stress environment. Shy, timid dogs will become more fearful. Dominant dogs will become pushier. Hyperactive dogs will live in a constant state of anxiety-fueled activity.

Remedial Training

Reluctance to Be Handled or Groomed

Breeders usually introduce their puppies to basic grooming at five weeks of age. Poorly socialized dogs may receive little or no exposure to grooming, and, as a result, become fearful of being handled. Your dog may begin showing signs of this as a puppy. In response to his complaints, his grooming may be neglected, allowing his aversion to grooming to intensify into full-blown fear by the time he reaches adolescence.

Repeated traumatizing experiences while being groomed can also create unpleasant associations, which can cause the dog to become defensive. When he suspects that grooming is imminent, he may attempt to run away or hide. He may cower and shake, with his ears pulled back, tail tucked, and teeth bared. Under these circumstances, he will need to be tranquilized or physically restrained for grooming, and it will be done as infrequently as possible, thus exacerbating the problem.

Desensitizing exercises are the only way to revise this behavior. This will require weeks of patient effort, but it is far preferable to a lifetime of anxious confrontations every time he must visit the veterinarian or groomer. Most dogs respond to a program of five minutes of daily desensitizing exercises. If you fear that your dog may bite, he should wear a head collar or muzzle

for these exercises. If you do not feel safe working with him, consult a behaviorist who has experience working with Poodles.

Introduce him to this program when he is quiet and relaxed. Sit on the floor with him, speak reassuringly, and offer a constant supply of tiny treats while using your other hand to gently massage him. Your goal is to create a positive association. Use a specific word as you handle each part of his body, and systematically reward him for cooperating. Constantly watch him for signs of fear or tension, and stop before he begins to object. Never admonish or restrain him, as this will put him on the defensive. Do not comfort him in an attempt to calm him; this will reinforce the unwanted response.

At first, avoid parts of his body that are likely to trigger a fearful reaction. Many dogs dislike having their feet or mouth handled. Gradually lengthen the sessions, and begin to touch his feet and examine his mouth. Once he has learned to tolerate systematic handling, use the same approach to familiarize him with each grooming procedure. Introduce him step by step to brushing, combing, and trimming. This may require months of short, positive reinforcement sessions. Be patient, and never push him to accept some-

BE PREPARED! Salvaging a Matted Coat

Rescue and shelter dogs rarely receive optimum coat care, and for Poodles, neglect often translates into serious matting. When confronting a badly matted coat, begin by assessing the dog's mental and physical condition and the coat texture. A harsh textured coat is easier to demat than a soft cottony coat. A nervous or elderly dog may not be able to cope with the stress of extensive dematting. This is an uncomfortable procedure no matter how gently it is done.

Always consider the dog's comfort first. If the coat is beyond hope, it may be more humane to shave the entire dog and concentrate on salvaging the ears, tail, and topknot. No dog should be expected to endure hours of dematting. No matter how dirty or flea infested the dog may be, never bathe a matted Poodle. The mats will shrink and become denser and tighter.

If the matting is not too extensive, use a mat splitting tool to break up the largest matted areas. Once they are a manageable size, they can be brushed. Give the dog frequent breaks and plenty of rewards during this process. Detangling products can also help to relax the hair and make it more slippery, so that the mats will brush out more easily.

thing before he is ready. Your goal is to always keep him below his panic threshold.

Recovery from this aversion does not mean that he has forgotten his fear or his accustomed response. Grooming must always be done with extreme patience and plenty of reassurance to prevent a relapse.

Housetraining

Housetraining lapses can have a myriad of causes. Most often, the dog was imperfectly trained to start with. As the existing problem becomes progressively worse, it simply becomes more noticeable. This is usually the case if the dog has a longstanding pattern of housetraining accidents, rather than a sudden change of habits. A trained dog will also let you know when he needs to go out rather than sneaking off to relieve himself in the corner. If the dog is accustomed to a schedule, and he is always taken out on time, make a point of remaining with him to ensure that he eliminates while he is out.

Cognitive dysfunction can also trigger housetraining problems. This may be the case for a senior dog who begins having accidents at random times and different locations throughout the home. This suggests that he is confused rather than following a habitual pattern. Housetraining lapses can also be caused by anxiety disorders like fear of separation. This may be the problem if the accidents are consistently associated with particular events, such as being left alone for the day. Excitement or submissive urination can be triggered by your return home. The arrival of a new dog in the home can prompt territorial urination in both intact and neutered dogs.

A range of medical issues should also be ruled out. Impaired sight or the pain of degenerative joint disease can make him reluctant to go out. Urinating in the house can also be attributed to diabetes, bladder stones, or kidney disease. Internal parasites can cause intermittent diarrhea.

For remedial housetraining, utilize the tried and true techniques of supervision, confinement, and reinforcement. Put him on a schedule, confine and supervise him closely, accompany him when he goes out to eliminate, stay with him until he does, and reinforce this behavior with praise and rewards. It may require six to eight weeks of strict retraining to instill new habits. During these weeks, block his access to all parts of the house that he has habitually used for a potty. Clean these areas thoroughly, which may include replacing rugs and drapes. Lingering odors will tempt him back into his former bad habits.

If most accidents occur at specific times, revise his elimination schedule to accommodate his body clock. Also consider revising his feeding schedule to ensure that he goes out to relieve himself within one hour of each meal.

Separation Anxiety

The term separation anxiety is used to explain or excuse a myriad of behavior problems that can be traced back to poor training. Genuine separation anxiety is an extreme reaction that occurs when a dog is separated from a particular individual or environment. Possible causes include generalized anxiety, excessive attachment to the owner, insufficient mental stimulation, or lack of acclimation to spending time alone. Poodles suffering from this disorder are usually neutered dogs acquired from a shelter or rescue, less than three years of age, and living with a single owner.

Separation anxiety is characterized by behavior like pacing, panting, whining, crying, vomiting, and/or diarrhea. The dog may hide to avoid being crated when he suspects that he will soon be left alone. When separated from his owner, he may refuse to eat, repeatedly attempt to escape by digging and scratching at doors and windows, engage in other destructive behavior, or obsessively lick and chew himself.

Follow these steps to revise separation anxiety:

- Place him in a safe, dog-proof enclosure whenever he is left alone.
- Do not respond to attention-seeking behavior, especially before leaving him alone. Use crates and gates to prevent him from following you around the house as you prepare to leave.
- Provide several interesting, interactive toys to keep him occupied in your absence. Make sure that he has sufficient daily exercise, but don't get him too keyed up with intensive exercise right before leaving him alone.
- Keep your departures low-key to minimize his anxiety level.

- Change your normal patterns in order to avoid giving him signals that you intend to depart. For instance, Poodles normally focus on cues like the sound of jingling keys.
- Ignore him for 15 minutes before you leave and after you return home. This will ensure that you do not inadvertently reinforce his anxious behavior associated with your arrivals and departures.
- It may also help to practice leaving him alone for five-or ten-minute periods throughout the day. Use a webcam to monitor his distress levels in your absence.
- Never leave him alone long enough to trigger a full-blown anxiety attack.
- Gradually increase the duration of separation as he learns to cope.
- If behavior modification fails, consider hiring a dog walker, or a dog sitter, or enrolling him in a daycare program to provide companionship in your absence. Some cases of separation anxiety respond to drug therapy.

Poodles with Disabilities

Vision Impairment
Unlike humans, most dogs usually learn to cope with visual impairment without much fuss. They live in the moment and do not spend time dwelling on their lost abilities or future difficulties. They simply adapt

by utilizing their other senses. For dogs, this is not too difficult, as their senses of hearing and smell rank far higher in their sensory repertoire. In many cases, Poodles refine their ability to cope with deteriorating vision long before their owners discover the disability.

If you realize that your dog is suffering from impaired vision, don't panic. Suddenly coddling him or radically changing his routine will not improve the situation. Direct your efforts to helping him cope. He has probably learned to navigate his way around familiar obstacles in your home. Poodles have good memories and easily formulate mental maps of their environment. Although he has probably learned to avoid danger spots, it is probably wise to block his access to stairs and rooms that contain possible hazards. Don't leave shoes, briefcases, or the vacuum cleaner in the middle of the floor. Sharp or dangerous items should be removed from his path. He may also become entangled in drapery cords or computer wires.

Most Poodles make a valiant effort to maintain their normal routine, so don't assume that he will suddenly realize that something is too difficult or dangerous. If he normally sits on the couch or sleeps on the bed, don't leave him on the furniture when you cannot supervise. If he is accustomed to leaping on and off without help, he may continue doing this despite the difficulty of successfully calculating a jump he cannot see.

You can use scents and sounds as landmarks to help him navigate in his familiar territory. For instance, keep the radio on in one room or add a recognizable scent to another. Wind chimes are a great auditory clue to help him find doorways. Avoid rearranging the rooms he frequents. This is

especially important when it comes to his water and favorite sleeping spots. His nose will help him find the food, but he may not drink enough if he has trouble locating his water dish.

If you have other pets, they should wear collar tags to advertise their whereabouts. A blind dog's food, treats, and chew toys should always be given to him in a crate. He will become more protective and prone to snap because he cannot read visual clues to determine the intentions of anyone approaching him. If he sleeps in a crate it will also alleviate the problem of sudden defensive aggression if he is awakened unexpectedly.

Along with a microchip, he should wear a collar with an ID tag that includes notification of his handicap. Gates must be kept securely shut. If he happens to wander out of your yard, he is at very high risk, so he will need closer supervision outdoors. He will be defenseless against stray dogs or predatory wildlife that may come into your yard. Give him a refresher course in basic obedience to reinforce his confidence. Add tactile signals to commands to tell him when to turn or slow down. These exercises will help him to sharpen his other senses.

Degenerative Joint Disease

Degenerative joint disease is a common complication of hip dysplasia and patellar luxation. Pain, stiffness, and limping usually become notice-able between ages five and eight as the cartilage protecting joints becomes brittle and wears away, leading to increasing pain and inflammation. These changes usually occur gradually, and you may attribute them to the inevi-table effects of old age rather than pain.

Many Poodles are quite stoic and manage to cope with pain until it becomes nearly debilitating. At that stage, your dog will exhibit obvious lameness and stiffness, especially after sleeping. He may refuse to climb stairs or navigate slippery floors. Males may begin squatting to urinate rather than lifting their legs. He may also favor one leg while standing, which will place additional stress on other joints and eventually compound the problem.

Most cases of degenerative joint disease can be managed with a combina-tion of pain medications and physical therapy. If your Poodle is overweight, put him on a diet. The stress of carrying excess weight has a direct impact on joint deterioration. His bed should be warm, soft, and comfortable to minimize joint stiffness.

Pain control will vastly improve his quality of life, as well as his overall health. Chronic pain will undermine his immune function, making him more susceptible to other diseases. Nonsteroidal anti-inflammatory drugs (NSAiDs) effectively control most cases of mild to moderate pain. Pain and stiffness often respond well to acupuncture. Massage therapy can also help to improve circulation and range of motion in sore joints and to loosen up painful, contracted muscles. Finally, swimming therapy is an excellent way to improve range of motion without placing additional stress on inflamed joints.

Resources

Books

Blome, Peter and Jeff Perry. *Disc Dogs! The Complete Guide*, Roswell, GA: Hyperflite, Inc. 2008

Dahl, Del. *The Complete Poodle*. New York: Howell Book House, 1994.

Donaldson, Jean. *The Culture Clash: A Revolutionary New Way of Understanding the Relationship Between Humans and Domestic Dogs*. Berkeley, CA: James & Kenneth, 1998.

Geeson, Eileen. *The Complete Standard Poodle*. New York: Howell Book House, 1998.

Massey, Gerald. *The Miniature Poodle*. London: Nicholson & Watson, 1964.

Pryor, Karen. *Reaching the Animal Mind: Clicker Training and What It Teaches Us About All Animals*. New York: Scribner, 2009.

Rogers, Alice Lang. *Poodles in Particular*. New York: Howell Book House, 1951.

Rooks, Robert DVM and Connie Jankowski. *Canine Orthopedics*. New York: Howell Book House, 1997.

Training and Behavior Websites

American College of Veterinary Behaviorists
www.veterinarybehaviorists.org

Animal Behavior Society
www.animalbehavior.org

Periodicals

AKC Gazette
gazette@akc.org
(800) 533-7323

AKC Family Dog
familydog@akc.org
(800) 533-7323

Top Notch Toys
Doll-McGinnis Publications
8848 Beverly Hills
Lakeland, FL 33809-1604
(863) 858-3839
www.dmcg.com/pubs/topnotchtoys/tnt_index.html

Dog World
P.O. Box 6500
Chicago, IL 60680
(800) 247-8080

Poodle Variety
P.O. Box 30430
Santa Barbara, CA 93130
(805) 963-9419
www.poodlevariety.com

Poodle Review
4401 Zephyr Street
Wheat Ridge, CO 80033
(303) 420-2222
www.hoflin.com

Health Websites

Merck Veterinary Manual
www.merckvetmanual.com

Canine Eye Registry Foundation
(CERF)
www.vmdb.org/cerf.html

Orthopedic Foundation for Animals
(OFA)
www.offa.org

Canine Health Information Center
(CHIC)
www.caninehealthinfo.org/

Poodle Activities
www.enchantedpoodleclub.com/
poodleactivities.htm

Dog Show Superintendents
www.infodog.com (MBF)
www.jbradshaw.com (Jack Bradshaw)
www.onofrio.com (Onofrio)
www.raudogshows.com (Jim Rau)
www.royjonesdogshows.com (Roy
Jones)
www.rogersdogshows.com (Rogers Dog
Shows)

Flyball
www.flyball.com

Disc Dogs
www.skyhoundz.com
www.iddha.com

Dock Diving
www.dockdogs.com

Hunting
www.outdoorchannel.com
www.akc.org/events/hunting_tests/
retrievers

American Kennel Club Good Citizen Program
www.akc.org/events/cgc/index.cfm

American Kennel Club Rally
www.akc.org/events/rally

American Kennel Club Obedience
www.akc.org/obedience

American Kennel Club Agility
www.akc.org/events.agility

North American Dog Agility Council
11522 S. Highway 3
Cataldo, ID 83810
www.nadac.com

United States Dog Agility Association
P.O. Box 850955
Richardson, TX 75085
(972) 487-2200
www.usdaa.com

Therapy Work
Delta Society Pet Partners Program
www.deltasociety.org
info@deltasociety.org
(425) 226-7357

Therapy Dogs International
(973) 252-9800
www.tdi-dog.org
tdi@gti.net

Therapy Dogs Incorporated
(877) 843-7364
www.therapydogs.com
therapydog@sisna.com

The Bright and Beautiful Therapy
Dogs, Inc.
(888) PET-5770
www.golden-dogs.org
info@golden-dogs.org

Poodle-Related Organizations

American Kennel Club
General Information
8051 Arco Corporate Drive, Suite 100
Raleigh, NC 27617-3390
(919) 233-9767
www.akc.org

United Kennel Club
100 East Kilgore Road
Kalamazoo, MI 49001
(616) 343-9020
www.ukcdogs.com

The Poodle Club of America
www.poodleclubofamerica.org

Rescue Poodle Information

www.akc.org/breeds/rescue
www.poodlerescuene.org
www.toypoodlerescue.net

Travel Information

USDA
*www.aphis.usda.gov/vs/ncie/iregs/
animals*

American Dog Owners Association
www.udoa.org

U.S. Department of Transportation
www.airconsumer.ost.dot.gov/reports
(for airline safety records regarding
animal loss, injury, or death)

American Kennel Club
*www.akc.org/public_education/travel_
tips.cfm*

Eileen's Directory of Pet-Friendly
Lodgings in the U.S. and Canada
www.travelpet.com
(800) 496-2665

www.Dogfriendly.com
(dog travel information and travel
guides, including free online
updates)
(877) 475-BARK (2275)

Online Pet Supply Retailers

www.carealotpets.com (general dog
supplies)
www.kingwholesale.com (general dog
supplies)
www.petedge.com (general dog
supplies)
www.ChrisSystems.com (grooming
supplies)

Information on Household Toxins

www.epa.gov
www.cdc.gov
www.eco-labels.org (for comparing
and understanding green labels)
www.aerias.org (for indoor air
quality)

Grooming Information

National Dog Groomers Association
www.nationaldoggroomers.com

www.findagroomer.com

Index

THE TEAM BEHIND THE *TRAIN YOUR DOG* DVD

Host **Nicole Wilde** is a certified Pet Dog Trainer and internationally recognized author and lecturer. Her books include *So You Want to Be a Dog Trainer* and *Help for Your Fearful Dog* (Phantom Publishing). In addition to working with dogs, Nicole has been working with wolves and wolf hybrids for over fifteen years and is considered an expert in the field.

Host **Laura Bourhenne** is a Professional Member of the Association of Pet Dog Trainers, and holds a degree in Exotic Animal Training. She has trained many species of animals including several species of primates, birds of prey, and many more. Laura is striving to enrich the lives of pets by training and educating the people they live with.

Director **Leo Zahn** is an award winning director/cinematographer/editor of television commercials, movies, and documentaries. He has directed and edited more than a dozen instructional DVDs through the Picture Company, a subsidiary of Picture Palace, Inc., based in Los Angeles.